THE GREENEST HOME

THE GREENEST HOME

Superinsulated and Passive House Design

Julie Torres Moskovitz

Princeton Architectural Press
New York

Published by
Princeton Architectural Press
37 East Seventh Street
New York, New York 10003

Visit our website at www.papress.com.

Editors: Nicola Brower and Jacob Moore
Designer: Jan Haux

Special thanks to: Sara Bader, Janet Behning, Fannie Bushin, Megan Carey,
Carina Cha, Andrea Chlad, Benjamin English, Russell Fernandez, Will Foster,
Jan Hartman, Diane Levinson, Jennifer Lippert, Katharine Myers, Margaret
Rogalski, Elana Schlenker, Dan Simon, Sara Stemen, Andrew Stepanian,
Paul Wagner, and Joseph Weston of Princeton Architectural Press
—Kevin C. Lippert, publisher

Library of Congress Cataloging-in-Publication Data
Torres Moskovitz, Julie, 1971–
The greenest home : superinsulated and passive house design /
Julie Torres Moskovitz. — First edition.
    pages cm
ISBN 978-1-61689-124-4 (hardcover : alk. paper)
1. Architecture, Domestic—Environmental aspects. 2. Architecture and
energy conservation. 3. Ecological houses. I. Title.
NA7117.3.T67 2013
728ʾ.047—dc23   2012030475

Front cover:

Passivhaus Vogel, Diethelm & Spillmann Architekten
Photo © Roger Frei and Diethelm & Spillmann Architekten

Back cover, top to bottom:

Orient Studio, Ryall Porter Sheridan Architects
Photo © Ty Cole

174 Grand, LoadingDock5
Photo © Raimond Koch

Hudson Passive Project, Dennis Wedlick Architect
Photo © Elliott Kaufman

Bamboo House, Karawitz Architecture
Photo © Herve Abbadie and Karawitz Architecture

R-HOUSE, ARO and Bernheimer Architecture
Photo © Richard Barnes

Tighthouse, Fabrica718
Photo © Hai Zhang

"*There is no way that we who have been caught in the meshes of the global economic web can go back to 'primitive' ways. We no longer have the possibility of developing unconscious behavior patterns that will lead to a restored and sustainable relationship with nature.... From here on we are doomed to consciousness. We must know, understand, be aware of, comprehend our relationships with the total biosphere on which our future depends.*"

—Raymond F. Dasmann
"Toward a Biosphere Consciousness,"
The Ends of the Earth: Perspectives on Modern Environmental History

CONTENTS

FOREWORD

Passive Houses are truly wonderful. They resonate so strongly because everything about them makes so much sense. It feels as if we have finally arrived at an energy efficiency standard that checks off all the boxes on energy use, year-round comfort, and indoor air quality. This integral approach has created a truly global community, since Passive House design has spread virally due to its reputation and proof of performance, and not because of branding or marketing. There is a buzz of excitement around Passive Houses that simply does not happen with other building standards. People talk about them in a wide-eyed way, marveling at the simplicity of the idea. Plain and simple, we are all hooked.

I fondly recall my first encounter with the Passive House concept, ten years ago at a conference in Tralee, Ireland. Hans Eek, a Swedish architect, was presenting one of his projects, recounting how, in the deep winter, a client contacted him to complain that the temperature in her Passive House was slowly dropping. After a little research, Eek discovered that the building's heating system had not been working for a full week! It took seven days of freezing cold weather for the client to notice that something was amiss. I was mesmerized, and on leaving the auditorium I called my wife immediately, and we decided to put our house on the market that very week. Two years later we moved into our own Passive House, the first certified project in the English-speaking world.

The Passive House standard can be applied to all sorts of building types. Schools, office buildings, athletic centers, and condos are all commonplace Passive House designs. Recent construction has included swimming pools, shopping malls, and even the world's first prison built to the Passive House standard. These innovations are being led by the brilliant building scientists at the Passive House Institute (PHI), under the leadership of physicist Dr. Wolfgang Feist, who has been working tirelessly for the past twenty years to push the boundaries and pave the way for the rest of the industry. In the last two years alone, PHI has introduced a globally accredited Passive House training program, a course for Passive House tradespersons, a worldwide retrofitting standard (EnerPHit), the International Passive House Association, updated Passive House Planning Package software, and more. Without question, Passive House design has nowhere to go but up.

The Passive House mentality is also driving innovation in the design and manufacture of building products themselves. The range of high-performance windows, ventilation systems, airtight materials, and thermal barrier solutions is ever expanding, creating much-needed green-collar employment in a sector that has been severely affected by the global recession. Companies are investing because they see energy-efficient construction as an inescapable part of the industry's future. For example, it was impossible to source triple-pane Passive House windows in Ireland ten years ago. Now there are at least three manufacturers of Passive House–certified windows, with others soon coming on board. The same can undoubtedly be expected worldwide as more and more people discover the importance of these products.

Julie Torres Moskovitz deserves heartfelt congratulations for this wonderful book, which will act as a catalyst for more widespread Passive House design and construction and inspire others just as I was inspired a decade ago. It is especially relevant in the United States, coming at an exciting time when momentum is building, knowledge is expanding, and more and more Passive House projects are being realized. This book celebrates those who have walked the walk—showing what can actually be achieved and illustrating that Passive House innovation is truly limitless.

I hope you will enjoy this inspiring book and join the Passive House party. I promise that you will not regret it.

Tomas O'Leary
Managing Director, Passive House Academy, Dublin, Ireland

ACKNOWLEDGMENTS

I am grateful to Princeton Architectural Press, especially editors Nicola Brower, Jacob Moore, and Sara Bader and designer Jan Haux.

Minyoung Song, Jade Yang, Kim Letven, and Taylor Wozniak were enthusiastic and helpful in pulling together this collection of important Passive House projects. Jordan Goldman was an excellent resource for editorial advice on building science. I thank Orlando Torres for his editorial work and Elio Torres for his patience with his mom's long work hours. I am grateful to Justin and Mamie for suggesting that we design a Passive House retrofit brownstone for them.

Without a doubt, the work of Wolfgang Feist and the PHI is a great contribution to our planet. Tomas O'Leary and the professionals at Passive House Academy are invaluable with their Passive House workshops and thermal-bridge trainings. Thanks also to Katrin Klingenberg of the PHIUS for sharing her own Passive House projects as case studies.

I am appreciative of Dr. Douglas B. Holmes for remembering 1979 as if it were yesterday and sharing his passive solar hybrid house with me. I am much obliged to the late architect William Mead, and to Hansi Mead and my mother, for handing me the 1982 *Technology Illustrated* article about Holmes's house the summer I started architecture school. I'm glad I hung on to it.

To all of the teams of pioneering and talented architects, engineers, scientists, builders, and clients working on Passive House projects—thank you, and keep it up.

Julie Torres Moskovitz

INTRODUCTION

Superinsulated and Passive House Design

The Passive House Standard

Simply said, a Passive House is a building that is very well insulated, virtually airtight, and primarily heated by the sun. It is designed to avoid excessive heat gain through shading and the placement of windows, so that little energy is needed by its occupants to either cool or heat the building. In fact, a Passive House can reduce heating energy consumption of its occupants by up to 90 percent and total energy consumption by 50 to 70 percent, in comparison with usage in a typical home. Although this book focuses on residential projects, the Passive House standard provides the road map to design all kinds of buildings—commercial, institutional, and even high-rise structures—that consume minimal amounts of energy.

There is always an infinite variation in individual building design, but to achieve this ultra-efficiency, Passive House designers rely on a set of common principles: insulate well and thoroughly, achieve airtightness, install high-performing windows for solar gain and sunscreens to avoid overheating, prevent thermal bridges, and provide constant fresh air through highly efficient heat recovery ventilation (HRV) systems. A compact building form and proper solar orientation also remain near the top of the list of considerations for maximizing energy efficiency.

Of course, human comfort plays a large role in the design as well. The interior temperature is optimized, designed to be approximately 68 degrees Fahrenheit with a comfortable relative humidity. In this controlled indoor environment, surfaces are close in temperature to that of the surrounding air. Cold spots and drafts that cause thermal discomfort—and

often lead to condensation or mold—are eliminated through air tightness and a continuous thermal envelope, while operable windows can be used for summer night cooling when humidity is low. A balance between a filtered fresh air supply and the extraction of exhaust air can even help minimize allergies and asthma.

While similar principles of sustainability have been used to design buildings for centuries, energy-modeling software and high-performance products now on the market have ushered in new levels of possible efficiency. European manufacturers in particular have developed many products to meet the demands of the Passive House standard, and North American companies are beginning to take note. The Passive House Planning Package (PHPP) energy-modeling software, developed by the Passive House Institute (PHI), founded in 1996 by the German physicist Wolfgang Feist, allows designers and builders to enter detailed information about their projects and to receive in return an instant analysis of how each component is working together and responding to the site conditions to create a low-energy house. The scientific design tool provides a way for architects to base their decisions on performance rather than mere aesthetics or general rules of thumb of energy efficiency. The software calculates energy data based on inputs such as local weather statistics, interior floor area, and thermal conductivity values of the materials used in the walls, roof, foundation slab, windows, and doors. The information provided by the PHPP enables the design team to quantify aspects of the design and to analyze the cost benefits of higher-performing materials over time. The modeling program accounts for solar gains as well as internal heat gains from equipment, light fixtures, and even body heat. These energy gains are added together and balanced with losses to calculate a building's annual space heating demand.

In the United States, architects can apply for Passive House certification through a PHI certifier, such as the Passive House Academy. EnerPHit certification—Quality-Approved Energy Retrofit with Passive House Components—is granted by PHI to existing buildings that are retrofitted to meet Passive House standards. (Since it is often difficult for retrofits to achieve all requirements needed for Passive House certification, the PHI has introduced this slightly relaxed standard to acknowledge improved energy performance of refurbished buildings.) Architects can also apply for PHIUS+ certification through the Passive House Institute US (PHIUS), a nonprofit organization distinct from PHI. To achieve Passive House certification, a building must meet a set of requirements:

—A certified Passive House must have an annual heating demand of not more than 4.75 kbtu/ft² per year (15 kWh/m² per year) and a cooling demand of not more than 4.75 kbtu/ft² per year (15 kWh/m² per year).

—The building's total primary energy consumption must not be more than 38 kbtu/ft² per year (120 kWh/m² per year).

—A Passive House must have an airtight building shell: Measured with a blower door, it must not leak more than 0.6 air changes per hour (ACH) when pressurized or depressurized to +/-50 pascals relative to outside. In other words, when the house is under test pressure conditions, six-tenths of the interior air volume will be replaced each hour. In a typical house the air is replaced six to ten times each hour under these test conditions, resulting in ten to seventeen times more air leakage.[1] Passive House designers usually undertake several blower-door tests during a project to determine if the minimum requirement for air tightness has been achieved.

In an airtight house, fresh air ventilation is crucial, so Passive Houses employ efficient HRV systems that provide fresh air to the house and exhaust stale air while recovering the heat from the exhausted air to preheat incoming fresh air during cold months.

Why Are Passive Houses Important?

According to Edward Mazria, director of the sustainable building advocacy organization Architecture 2030, "What we need is a paradigm shift in the way we view energy consumption in this country. It's architecture—residential, commercial, and industrial buildings and their construction materials—that accounts for nearly half of all energy used in this country each year. And it's the architects who hold the key to turning down the global thermostat."[2] At a time when climate change is of increasing concern, Architecture 2030 is geared to helping the building sector move toward carbon neutrality by the year 2030.[3] The organization challenges the building industry to design and build in ways that acknowledge these statistics and limit climate change, stating that "by the year 2035, approximately 75 percent of the built environment (in the United States) will be either new or renovated," an opportunity that should not be missed.[3] All eighteen case studies included in this book are committed to this path to carbon neutrality and indicate possible ways to achieve this goal.

Passive Houses Today

According to the 16th International Passive House Conference, held in May of 2012 in Hanover, Germany, more than forty thousand Passive House projects had been built worldwide as of that year.[4] In the early 2000s PHI studied 114 residential Passive House apartments in five European countries, determining that there was an average of 90 percent savings on energy consumption as compared with the typical European home.[5] As adherence to Passive House standards spreads worldwide, PHI continues to conduct research and to update its energy-modeling software to incorporate new findings, such as varying needs for cooling and dehumidification based on differing climate conditions. In 2012 PHI started working on a program called PassREg, which was created to support projects that not only meet Passive House standards but also incorporate renewable energy technologies to achieve a level of net zero energy or even feed back into the energy grid.[6] These Energy Plus homes, three of which are discussed in the following chapters (Bamboo, Vogel, and Textile Houses), produce more energy per year than they consume.

One of the strongest commitments to Passive House principles is the target the European Parliament has set for all new buildings to be nearly zero energy buildings (nZEB) by 2020.[7] (By the end of 2012 European Union member states will provide a definition for nZEBs, including specific targets per building category.[8]) Some areas of Germany have already established that all new construction must meet Passive House standards. This book is meant to inspire a worldwide public and to show that these kinds of goals are within our collective reach. While relatively few Passive House buildings exist in the United States today, the number of its advocates and clients interested in energy-efficient buildings is constantly growing.

The clients, architects, builders, and manufacturers featured in this book are pioneers in this movement toward low-energy consumption, and they have taken a giant leap toward creating a society that is in better balance with the planet. While a building must first be designed to meet Passive House standards, contractors and subcontractors play a critical role as well, because the airtightness and thermal envelope of these buildings depend on thorough attention to detail during construction. Fortunately, Passive House–certified consultants, designers, and tradesmen can today be found virtually everywhere.

Still, there is room for growth in the North American green building industry for Passive House products. Currently, the windows, doors, efficient ventilation systems, and high-performance tapes and membranes needed for Passive House construction are much more readily available in Europe, where the Passive House standard was first codified. In these countries there is even a certification process for products, not only for buildings. Presently, there is tremendous potential for North American manufacturers to develop and sell their own high-performance products. The case studies featured in this book describe two of the new companies that have been established or redirected as Passive House interest has grown in North America: a company manufacturing preassembled Passive House panels outside Vancouver, British Columbia, and a plant fabricating modular elements for Passive House buildings in the greater Philadelphia area. In addition, the Hudson Passive Project, which broke US airtightness records in 2010, relied on structural insulated panels and beams produced by a Vermont company.

Early American Passive Solar and Superinsulated Homes

In the United States the oil embargoes of 1973 and 1974 led to increased energy conservation, and experimentation in alternative-energy technologies and low-energy residential design. The energy crisis of 1979 further highlighted how dependent the US economy was on imported fossil fuels, leading President Jimmy Carter to proclaim on July 15: "Beginning this moment, this nation will never use more foreign oil than we did in 1977—never. From now on, every new addition to our demand for energy will be met from our own production and our own conservation."[9] In this milieu of urgency, there was a palpable interest in scientific design strategies, building science, and the potential of alternative energy. In 1978 the American Institute of Architects claimed, "If the U.S. adopted a high-priority national

program emphasizing energy efficient buildings, we could by 1990 be saving the equivalent of more than 12.5 million barrels of petroleum per day."[10]

Not coincidentally, then, during the 1970s and 1980s there were many homes being built and studied in the United States and Canada that employed principles of passive solar design, were superinsulated, or were what Harvard physicist Dr. William A. Shurcliff called Double-Envelope Houses.[11] Some of these buildings were, in essence, prefiguring Passive Houses, combining the principles of passive solar design and superinsulation. These case studies and the detailed reports provided about them were pivotal in helping inform the physicists Bo Adamson and Feist's development of the Passive House concept in 1988.[12] Unfortunately, the vibrant movement's progress, as well as its calls for energy conservation, waned as the price of oil decreased again during the late 1980s and early 1990s.

An early hybrid house combining passive solar design and thorough insulation was prominently featured in the January 1982 issue of *Technology Illustrated*. Located in Lexington, Massachusetts, the residence was designed in 1980 by the Harvard-educated architect William Mead, in collaboration with the owner, Dr. Douglas B. Holmes, an engineer trained at the Massachusetts Institute of Technology (MIT) and the Delft University of Technology in the Netherlands. Holmes, who was passionately involved in nearly every detail of his home's design, still lives in the house to this day and jokes that for the past thirty-two years, "heating his home has cost him less than half a cord of wood a winter."[13]

The Passive·Solar House

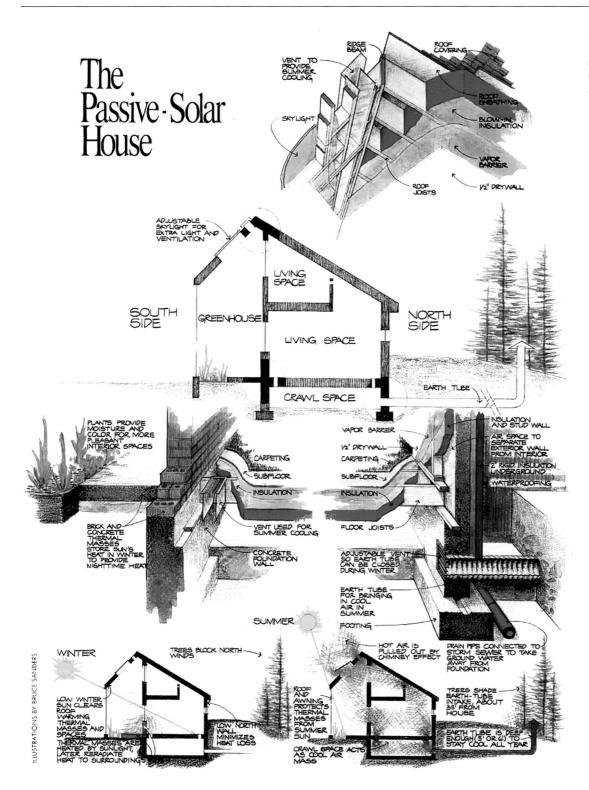

ILLUSTRATIONS BY BRUCE SANDERS

LEFT: **Illustration from** *Technology Illustrated* **magazine of Holmes's passive solar hybrid home in Lexington, Massachusetts, circa 1982**

LEFT: **The Saskatchewan Conservation House, built in 1978, was a superinsulated home that, after its completion, received thousands of curious visitors.**

importantly, it is a real road map for a new relationship with the planet.

To encourage readers to contemplate man's global positioning and interconnectedness, the ordering of the projects in this book is purposefully based on each building's angular distance from the equator, or latitude. In 1954 Buckminster Fuller, the architect and inventor who worked across disciplines to promote human development, completed his Dymaxion map of the Earth, exhibited in this book's project list.[23] In Fuller's map the continents are presented as one continuous island, which seems appropriate given the broad applicability of Passive House design and its implications for addressing climate change worldwide. The studies included in the following chapters, along with the detailed project characteristics that follow, are presented as inspiration and encouragement to all those people interested in marrying good design with truly achievable and necessary sustainability.

1   Jordan Goldman, Passive House consultant and mechanical engineer, in discussion with author, July 2012.

2   Edward Mazria, "It's the Architecture, Stupid!," *Solar Today* (May–June 2003), 49.

3   "Solution: The Building Sector," Architecture 2030, accessed August 09, 2012, http://www.architecture2030.org/the_solution/buildings_solution_how.

4   Passive House Institute, "Master Plan for the European Energy Revolution Put Forth," press release (Hanover, Germany: 16th International Passive House Conference, May 9, 2012).

5   "What is a Passive House?" International Passive House Association, accessed August 09, 2012, http://www.passipedia.passiv.de/passipedia_en/basics/what_is_a_passive_house.

6   International Passive House Association, Research, *iPHA Newsletter* 6 (Hanover, Germany: Spring 2012), 6.

7   "Commissioner Piebalgs Welcomes Political Agreement on Energy Performance of Buildings," Communication Department of the European Commission, accessed August 09, 2012, http://europa.eu/rapid/pressReleasesAction.do?reference=IP/09/09/1733, Press Release (Brussels, Belgium: November 18, 2009).

8   European Climate Foundation, "EU 'Nearly Zero-Energy Building' Targets Announced for 2020," accessed August 09, 2012, http://www.europeanclimate.org/en/news/93-eu-qnearly-zero-energy-buildingq-targets-announced-for-2020.

9   President's Address to the Nation on Energy and National Goals, 2 Pub. Papers 1235 (July 15, 1979).

10 American Institute of Architects, "A Nation of Energy Efficiency Buildings by 1990." Washington, D.C.: AIA, 1975.

11 William A. Shurcliff, *Super Insulated Houses and Double Envelope Houses* (Andover, MA: Brick House, 1981), 3.

12 "Passive House-Historical Review?" International Passive House Association, accessed August 09, 2012, http://www.passipedia.passiv.de/passipedia_en/basics/the_passive_house_-_historical_review.

13 Douglas Holmes, home owner, engineer, and physicist, in discussion with author, September 2011.

14 David Holzman, "Is Passive Solar Passe?," *Illustrated Technology*, December–January 1982, 37.

15 Ibid., 40.

16 R. O. Stromberg and S. O. Woodall, "Passive Solar Buildings: A Compilation of Data and Results," Solar Technical Liaison Division 5714, Sandia Laboratories: Albuquerque, NM, SAND77-1204, 28–30.

17 Donald W. Aitken, "The 'Solar Hemicycle' Revisited: It's Still Showing the Way," *Wisconsin Academy Review*, Winter 1992–93, 33.

18 Ibid., 33–37.

19 William A. Shurcliff, *Super Insulated Houses and Air-to-Air Heat Exchangers* (Andover, MA: Brick House, 1988), 22.

20 Ibid., 23.

21 Nancy Rubin, "Blankets of Air Heat Solar House," *New York Times*, October 14, 1979.

22 Ibid.

23 "Dymaxion Map," Buckminster Fuller Institute, accessed August 09, 2012, http://bfi.org/about-bucky/buckys-big-ideas/dymaxion-world/dymaxion-map.

PROJECTS

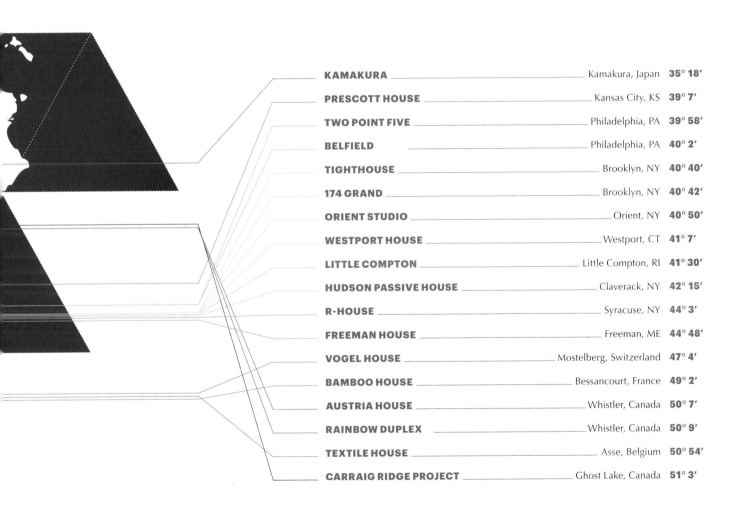

KAMAKURA

The first Japanese Passive House was built in Kamakura, about thirty miles southwest of Tokyo. Completed in 2009, the house is located in a quiet residential neighborhood in a town best known for its historic temples and scenic coastline. According to Miwa Mori of Key Architects, particularly since the Fukushima Daiichi nuclear accident in 2011, the Japanese public has become increasingly interested in building homes that consume less energy.[1] Mori and her business partner, Joerg Heil, studied and worked for many years in Germany on energy-efficient buildings before designing the Kamakura house, one of the first projects taken on by their practice after its relocation to Tokyo.

Most of Japan, including the prefecture of Kanagawa where Kamakura is located, has a humid subtropical climate, which poses special challenges for a Passive House. Traditional Japanese architecture already makes use of passive cooling through such elements as south-facing windows with deep roof overhangs. Clay walls supply thermal mass and help manage humidity, while sliding screens allow for cross ventilation. A main concern with an airtight construction is mold caused by moisture, but Key Architects studied the balance required to address the seasonal fluctuations in humidity and included a smart vapor barrier in the building assembly.

The Kamakura House is on a small site with little space for a yard, but the designers did incorporate one small exterior space at the entry, used for removing shoes before crossing the threshold—an important Japanese custom. In lieu of a landscape garden at ground level, as found in other traditional homes

in the neighborhood, this house has a roof terrace on which the client has now planted a vegetable garden. The minimalist facade is defined by an elegant, floating, white ship's ladder stair that leads directly, from the upper-level living spaces to the roof terrace. On the front of the house, a corner window for the home office provides views of the hillside and a small nearby river.

Key Architects's greatest challenge with this project was merging seismic code requirements with Passive House standards. Of note is the southern facade, which in Passive House buildings usually features large areas of high-performance glazing that allow for solar gains. In this dwelling, however, the size of the window openings had to be limited because of seismic code constraints. The solution, then, was to strategically position the windows to make the best use of light. The facade assembly features a ventilated rainscreen of charcoaled cedar backed by 2x6 wood framing in-filled with wood timber insulation. The wall's interior side is covered with an intelligent membrane, secured with air-sealing tape, that offers low-vapor permeability in the winter and high-vapor permeability in the summer. This allows the airtight wall to remain dry during changing moisture conditions throughout the year. A service cavity, located in front of the insulated wall and concealed with plasterboard, provides space for electrical lines without disrupting the wall's air barrier and continuous thermal insulation. The charcoaled cedar boards used for the exterior cladding are traditional and highly resistant to moisture and insects, and the windows, imported from Germany,

35° 18′

Kamakura, Japan

Key Architects

2009

Certified by PHI

OPPOSITE: The overhang at the Kamakura House defines the entry area on this narrow lot. There is limited space at the ground level for landscaping, so the architects instead included an area above for a roof garden.

are Passive House certified. The foundation slab is insulated with extruded polystyrene foam (XPS) boards and concrete screed topping. The interior of the house features natural materials, such as tongue-and-groove bamboo flooring and common-place bamboo cabinetry in both the kitchen and the office.

The mechanical system in the Kamakura House is simple and includes an HRV to provide fresh air, an air source heat pump (ASHP) for heating and cooling, and a heat pump for hot water. There is no gas service to the building.

Key Architects is committed to building energy-efficient buildings that are earthquake-proof for Japan, and the firm gives presentations and leads workshops on Passive House concepts. So far, Key Architects is the only Passive House–certified consultant in Japan, but the partners explain that, despite this lack of certification, the country has an active Passive House group with almost one hundred members. Since the completion of the Kamakura House, Mori and Heil have been busy working on several other Passive House residences as well as larger-scale Passive House projects, such as a new Zen temple in central Tokyo.

1 Miwa Mori, interview by Kirsten Priebe, "Passive House around the Globe," video, Fifteenth International Passive House Conference, June 2011, www.arcreation.co.uk.

OPPOSITE LEFT: **The structural attachments for the white ship's ladder were designed to provide a thermal break.**

OPPOSITE RIGHT: **The corner detail highlights the craftsmanship that was required at the window reveals of the charcoaled cedar panels.**

BELOW: **The south-facing entry includes a stone platform underneath the overhang for guests to remove their shoes before entering.**

BELOW: The south facade has windows for solar gain, but the size of the openings was limited by seismic code prescriptions. The corner window provides views of the hillside from the second-floor home office.

BELOW: The roof terrace features block pavers and grass at the corners that hide large drains.

ACCORDING TO MIWA MORI of Key Architects, particularly since the Fukushima Daiichi nuclear accident in 2011, the Japanese public has become increasingly interested in building homes that consume less energy.

LEFT: **The Passive House–certified windows were imported from Germany and feature an easy-to-use tilt-and-turn mechanism, allowing the windows to tilt in or open as casements.**

TOP RIGHT: **View of the open kitchen area that looks on to the play area and the dining room. A simple soffit provides the supply and exhaust grilles for the fresh air ventilation system.**

BOTTOM RIGHT: **The corner window is installed on the interior of the wall assembly to allow for an exterior overhang that prevents overheating.**

1 MASTER BEDROOM
2 MASTER BATHROOM
3 CHILDREN'S ROOM 1
4 CHILDREN'S ROOM 2
5 WC
6 LIVING SPACE
7 KITCHEN
8 DINING ROOM
9 HOME OFFICE

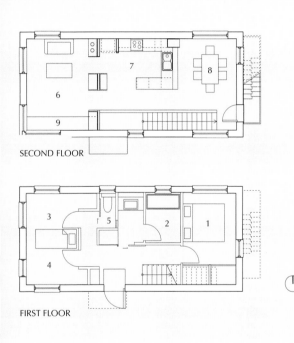

SECOND FLOOR

FIRST FLOOR

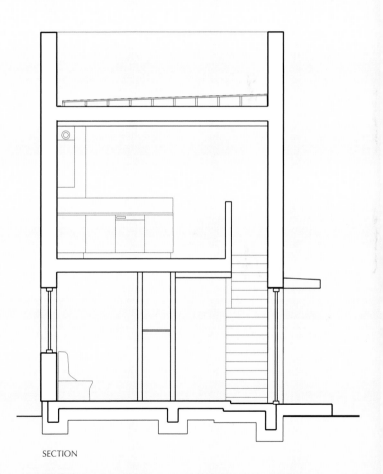

SECTION

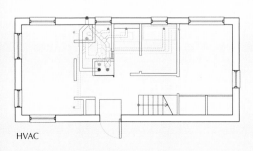

HVAC

PRESCOTT HOUSE

Studio 804 is a nonprofit corporation and a design/build course taught at the University of Kansas School of Architecture by Dan Rockhill. During the past sixteen years of its existence, Studio 804, which specializes in sustainable architecture, has not only built the first LEED platinum-certified building in Kansas—the 547 Arts Center in Greensburg, which was also the first public project completed in 2008, the year after a tornado decimated the town—but also designed and built the Prescott House, a LEED platinum-certified building and the first Passive House project in the state. Since construction was completed in May 2010, the students of Studio 804 have raised funds for, designed, and built two more Passive Houses in Kansas.

The 1,700-square-foot Prescott House is a single-family home located in the Prescott neighborhood of Kansas City. Each year Studio 804 works in a different area of the state, in this case an urban transitional neighborhood with stand-alone homes. The Prescott House takes a simple, compact form with a gabled roof and is small by Kansas standards. Its double-height living room with open loft space is atypical of the homes in the region but allows for good air circulation. The small footprint is not only more energy-efficient but also leaves room for more landscaped areas on the hilly property.

The site's slope led students to design entries to the house on two different ground planes. They also opted for a carport in lieu of a traditional garage, which enabled them to add an open exterior deck similar in scale to neighboring porches. The house's handsome rainscreen system is made of charred Douglas fir. The students spent long hours perfecting the finish on this durable material.

Rockhill describes his studio's efforts as a push for good design and sustainability. His students analyzed how natural ventilation could occur from positioning windows in specific locations, but they found that Kansas summers are so hot and humid, even at night, that it is hard to find a good breeze. The high humidity in this setting works against night cooling and, in fact, creates interior discomfort. As a result, active cooling makes more sense here than in other climates.

As Rockhill has learned over the years, the designer's ideal of giving owners flexibility with building elements, such as operable louvers and window devices, is not always the best solution in reality. The louvers on the south-facing facade of the Prescott House are a prime example. External sunshades are imperative on a Passive House and must be installed at a specific angle to block out the heat from the summer sun yet allow the maximum amount of light to enter when the sun is low during the winter. Rockhill led his students to the design of fixed louvers rather than create flexibility for the owners that could allow for misuse. As the professor explains, if residents have the option of manipulating items they do not necessarily understand, the house's energy consumption can be greatly compromised.

The Prescott House is built of TJI joists, an engineered wood product that contains deep cavities for densely-packed cellulose insulation. The students added nine inches of rigid insulation underneath the first-floor concrete slab, which radiates the heat

39° 7'

Kansas City, Kansas

Studio 804

2010

Certified by PHIUS

OPPOSITE: **Studio 804 accommodated the hilly site by designing two distinct entry levels and berming the lower portion of the building into the hillside.**

1 STORAGE
2 LAUNDRY
3 FLEX SPACE
4 CARPORT
5 FLEX SPACE
6 BEDROOM
7 BATHROOM
8 KITCHEN
9 LIVING ROOM
10 PORCH
11 FLEX SPACE
12 BATHROOM
13 BEDROOM

BELOW: **Section looking west. Concrete thermal mass and TJI structural panels provided deep cavities for insulation at the walls and roof.**

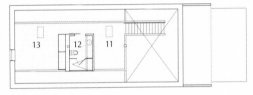

LOFT LEVEL

MAIN LEVEL

BASEMENT

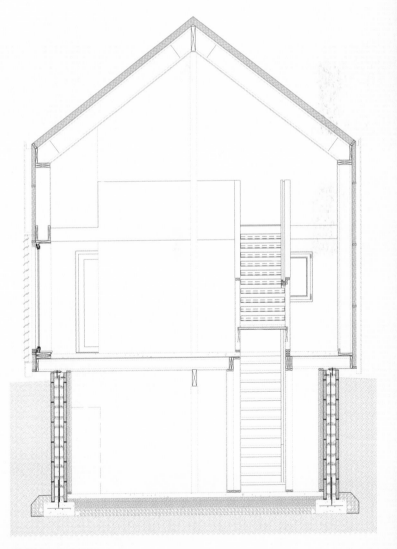

SECTION

TWO POINT FIVE

The Two Point Five house, a single-family model home named for its two-and-a-half floors, is the fourth collaborative project designed by ISA (Interface Studio Architecture) for the developer Postgreen in an ongoing series of in-fill urban residential construction that is both economical and eco-friendly. Postgreen seeks out vacant lots that are near the Spring Garden stop of the Frankford El train line in northeast Philadelphia in the up-and-coming neighborhood East Kensington. This section of Philadelphia is often affectionately referred to as the sixth borough of New York City, but there is one notable difference: vacant lots here are abundant and affordable. In addition, the city's Licensing and Inspections Department and the Water Department are supportive of the green and innovative projects being developed throughout Philadelphia, particularly in the neighborhoods northeast of Northern Liberties. This area is clearly in transition, with developers and new businesses investing substantial amounts of money locally. More and more colorful new in-fill projects are juxtaposed with the monotonous grid of midcentury brick row houses.

The collaboration between ISA and Postgreen, which includes the 100K House, the Skinny House, the Passive House, and the Two Point Five House, has been an interesting balancing act between affordability and innovative and interesting design. For example, while each Postgreen building is clad with a cement-board rainscreen, ISA attempts to offer a fresh interpretation of this material through investigations in color, texture, and scale. Chad Ludeman, president of Postgreen, stepped into the role of

contractor during the course of the four building projects. A manufacturing engineer by training, he quickly recognized the need for careful sequencing and quality detailing when building to Passive House standards. Disappointed with the work of local contractors—such as an experience when a subcontractor inadvertently cut through a wall's continuous air barrier—it seemed natural for him to become a contractor himself.

The developer caters to home buyers looking for new urban houses that are both responsibly built and affordable. The firm's website enables clients to easily consider various sustainable options and spatial layouts through a menu that allows them to select everything from solar thermal and solar photovoltaic panels to the size of the house and the type of green finish materials used.

Starting with their first project in the neighborhood, the well-known 100K House, Postgreen and ISA decided that new construction was easier to build to a high standard of energy efficiency than retrofitting the city's existing housing stock. All of the firms' house developments are built on multiple and adjacent properties, since there is relative efficiency in this approach. Before breaking ground for the 100K home, ISA and Postgreen studied different construction methods and material assemblies to determine the most affordable options. Ever since their first model house was completed, they have learned from each new project, and their experience has allowed them to perfect building assemblies and detailing. They commenced with an eight-inch structural insulated panel (SIP), then tested twelve-inch SIPs, before

39° 58′

Philadelphia, Pennsylvania

ISA and Postgreen

2011

Not certified

OPPOSITE: Southwest elevation of the Two Point Five House

finally deciding on double-stud walls. They use a ZIP system, which is composed of a structural engineered wood panel with a water-resistive barrier, to ensure a continuous air barrier and are now well versed in making efficient use of gaskets and tapes. The patterning of the rainscreen used for the homes' facades varies depending on the size of the window modules and reflects experiments in composition and color. The firms have also experimented with solar shading devices, as seen in the aluminum shields of the Skinny House and the deep inset windows of the Two Point Five House.

The Two Point Five House reflects the accumulated knowledge of previous projects and is not only expertly detailed but also features several special elements, including solar thermal panels for hot water and a roof terrace off the master bedroom. The facade's cement-board rainscreen boasts a clever zippered black-panel pattern. The interior layout includes a first-floor plan with no interior dividing walls and an open kitchen, which allows for the HRV supply and exhaust system to easily and efficiently circulate fresh air. The second floor combines a bedroom and bathroom with a large flexible space, and the top floor holds a private master bedroom suite. The interior is more sophisticated than that of the earlier 100K House, which is raw and industrial. The Two Point Five House's prefinished black bamboo flooring and drywall, instead of exposed plywood, result in a look that the architects refer to as "100K lux." The kitchen cabinets are custom-made and formaldehyde-free, and the Cambria countertops are the only quartz counters fabricated in the United States.

The building's airtight envelope starts at the first-floor level with cellulose blown in between the floor joists. The cellar houses the HRV system and is outside the insulated envelope, which made it necessary for the architects to design special detailing for the stair enclosure to keep the envelope airtight. The insulated cellar door has perimeter gaskets, and the base of the staircase rests on an insulated concrete pad. Other sustainable details include amenities for rain collection, energy monitoring, and triple-pane windows.

As the Two Point Five House shows, both ISA and Postgreen have made a science of balancing economic considerations with design elements while helping define a demographic of young homeowners who are proud to be part of this forward-thinking green venture.

LEFT: **The Skinny House was designed to meet optimum value engineering (OVE) framing. All wall studs and floor joists are twenty-four inches on center rather than the typical sixteen inches. Windows and cladding are coordinated with stud spacing for greater material efficiency and less overall construction waste.**

RIGHT: **In a play on its standard cement-board rainscreen system, ISA worked with a local print-screen artist to develop a pixilated cloud pattern for the Skinny House facade and a custom fixed shading device for the windows.**

BELOW: **The 100K House is the first in a series of energy-efficient homes that are based on Passive House principles.**

BELOW: **This view of the roof terrace shows the wide covering over the thick, highly insulated facade.**

BELOW: The open kitchen of the Two Point Five House, as part of a second-floor plan with no interior dividing walls, allows for the HRV supply and exhaust system to easily and efficiently circulate fresh air.

AS THE TWO POINT FIVE HOUSE SHOWS, both ISA and Postgreen have made a science of balancing economic considerations with design elements while helping define a demographic of young homeowners who are proud to be a part of this forward-thinking green venture.

TOP LEFT: **The 100K House explores the balance between eco-friendly and cost-effective decision making. Exposed concrete floors and unfinished laminated plywood stairs exemplify the firms' modern industrial aesthetic.**

BOTTOM LEFT: **Featuring simple, raw, industrial finishes for its young, urban clientele, the material palette also allowed Postgreen to direct more of its budget for the 100K House toward the building envelope.**

RIGHT: **Laminated plywood stringer and treads in the 100K House**

1 KITCHEN
2 LIVING ROOM
3 OPEN TO BELOW
4 BEDROOM
5 BATHROOM WITH
  WASHER / DRYER
6 FLEX SPACE
7 MASTER TERRACE
8 MASTER BATHROOM /
  DRESSING
9 MASTER BEDROOM

BELOW: **Map highlighting the first four collaborative projects between ISA and Postgreen in the East Kensington neighborhood of Philadelphia**

THIRD FLOOR

SECOND FLOOR

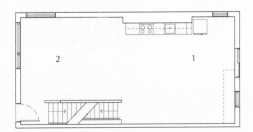

FIRST FLOOR

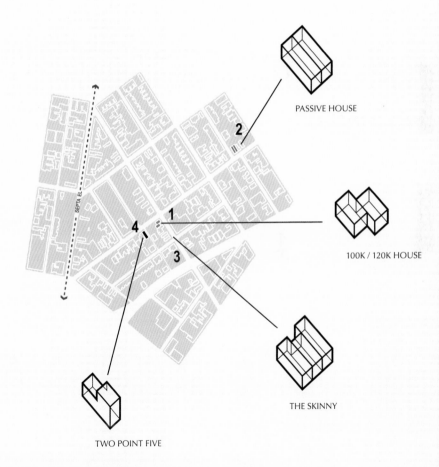

PASSIVE HOUSE

100K / 120K HOUSE

THE SKINNY

TWO POINT FIVE

BELFIELD

Onion Flats is a design-build firm based in Philadelphia that welcomes challenging sustainable projects. When Habeeba Ali asked the architects to design affordable eco-friendly townhouses for her nonprofit association Raise of Hope, which provides housing to formerly homeless and low-income families, they embraced the opportunity despite the tight schedule of the project. The partners, three brothers and a childhood friend, knew they could design and build the houses as modular Passive Houses within the five months required to qualify for the project's federal funding. Ali, who has been an advocate for homeless rights after she herself had been homeless for a time with her four children, lives just a few blocks from the association's first ground-up project, the Belfield Avenue townhouse development in northeast Philadelphia's Logan community.

The three townhouses making up the development are rental units, designed to help large families transition from the shelter housing system. The homes are handicap-accessible and feature four bedrooms and a home office. In addition to offering housing, the organization provides social services to tenants that include GED training, school tutoring, and substance abuse prevention counseling. Ali's late husband acquired the lots for the development in 2002, but it took many years of perseverance and dedication to secure full funding for the project from the Philadelphia Redevelopment Authority.

The Belfield Avenue project is a Passive House complex that is virtually off the grid, since the sun provides most of the energy needed to heat the buildings. Not only does the community benefit from the affordable housing, but this development also shows the potential of sustainable architecture in the twenty-first century. Onion Flats, who codeveloped this project, has been leading the eco-friendly redevelopment of northeast Philadelphia for the past ten years. The firm's experience in the field has allowed its partners to experiment with all types of detailing and sustainable features in their large-scale residential projects while establishing their own companies for design-build, modular construction, green roofs, and solar installation. The Belfield Avenue complex provided the perfect opportunity for the firm to expand on its vision, and they now have over 250 units of Passive House projects in the works around the Philadelphia area .

The Belfield townhouses became Onion Flats's first modular Passive House buildings. Each module was prefabricated at Onion Flats's local facility, with its structure, electric and monitoring systems, plumbing, and finishes preinstalled. The architects built as much as possible in the factory; while the houses' brick sidings were installed after the modules were set in place, the units themselves were clad with metal-finish panels before they left for the building site, except for a twelve-inch gap where seam connections had to be made on-site.

Building off-site in a controlled environment allows the firm to carefully oversee each component and check it for quality. A subcontractor unfamiliar with Passive House standards can, for example, easily cut through a critical layer of material to carve out space for an electrical conduit, thus destroying

40° 2′

Philadelphia,
Pennsylvania

Onion Flats

2012

Certified by PHI

OPPOSITE: **Each townhouse has a 5kW array which is often enough to provide an energy surplus and to feed back to the power grid bringing the project to net zero.**

airtight and insulated layers. A factory-built module helps guarantee that the wall, slab, and ceiling assemblies remain airtight and that the insulation is applied correctly and thoroughly. The townhouses' modular assembly consists of 2 x 6 foot wood stud walls filled with dense-packed cellulose for insulation, a wall sheathing with an integral air and moisture barrier, and a final exterior layer of two-inch-thick polyisocyanurate (polyiso) board insulation and metal cladding.

Each rental unit has a large front stoop and porch to encourage social interaction with neighbors, as well as a custom green grow wall for privacy. The homes also each have their own yard and parking area, and their roofs are maximized for solar power collection (each with 5kW). Sun studies led Onion Flats to design fixed shading devices at the southwest facade elevation to block the late-afternoon summer sun. The unit interiors provide ample space, with five bedrooms and even a laundry room on the second floor. Finish materials are simple so that renters can individualize their space, but kitchens include IKEA cabinetry, and the tiled bathrooms feature vessel sinks custom-made by a local artisan.

BELOW: Each unit has its own rear yard, and the adjacent land to the north features a triangular-shaped common area with a community garden.

As part of the construction, Onion Flats worked with consultants to develop a dashboard system that collects data and studies the townhouses' performances. One reason to study such data is to ensure that the rental units are operating efficiently for tenants. Monitoring Passive Houses and sharing their performance records is also important because it allows the public to learn how efficiently these buildings operate. The data collected for the Belfield Avenue Townhouse Development includes information on electrical usage, solar power collected, temperature and humidity levels, and air-quality levels.

Raise of Hope's townhouses bring hope to urban neighborhoods around the world that combining affordability and sustainability is possible.

EACH MODULE WAS PREFABRICATED at Onion Flats's *local facility, with its structure, electric and monitoring systems, plumbing, and finishes preinstalled. The architects built as much as possible in the factory.*

TOP RIGHT: **Street-level first floor, which features the kitchen and living area with ample natural light**

BOTTOM RIGHT: **The staircase in each townhouse unit features a custom-milled wood panel with a perforation pattern.**

1 BEDROOM
2 BATHROOM
3 KITCHEN
4 PORCH
5 LAUNDRY ROOM
6 MECHANICAL ROOM
7 OFFICE

THIRD FLOOR

SECOND FLOOR

FIRST FLOOR

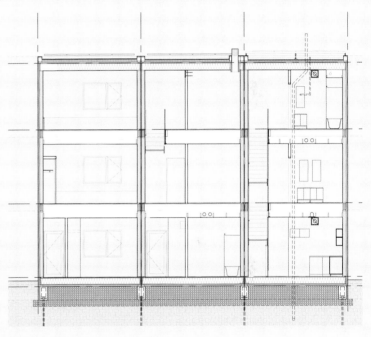

SECTION

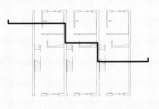

TIGHTHOUSE

Brooklyn is a hub of innovative architecture and design. Dozens of young professionals are commissioning or undertaking their own eco-sensitive renovations to existing brownstones and low-rise attached buildings throughout the borough. Tighthouse is centrally located off of Fifth Avenue in the neighborhood of Park Slope. This Passive House retrofit brownstone sits at the end of a string of two-story buildings constructed in 1899 that share a tree-lined block with larger brownstones built around the same time. It is the first certified Passive House in New York City and meets the standards for new construction, surpassing the EnerPHit certification.

The unique retrofit of a 110-year-old house by the Brooklyn-based firm Fabrica718 could serve as an important model for the many urban and suburban residences that need energy-saving renovations. Much more so than new construction, each Passive House retrofit involves its own singular set of conditions that demand creative problem solving and meticulous attention to insulation.

The owners of Tighthouse, a young couple from Ohio, considered the long-term benefits of a low-energy Passive House and understood that this gut renovation was a unique opportunity to comprehensively insulate their building. It is no wonder that the clients, who grew up in an age of smartphones and have little tolerance for inefficiency, were attracted to the idea of a Passive Home, which is nothing other than a smart and innovative machine for living. The couple's Midwestern pragmatism helped set the stage for finding efficient solutions to every aspect of the renovation, including the lighting, audiovisual, security, and mechanical systems.

The growing family required slightly more space than the brownstone's original plan provided. Fortunately, local zoning regulations permitted the architects to add an additional story to the building. The new penthouse added enough space to include an art studio for the husband in the building's basement. The top-floor master bedroom is defined by the new roof's bold angles, sloping twenty-one degrees and oriented along the north-south axis. This tilted and turned roof was designed to maximize exposure to the light and heat of the sun for solar thermal and photovoltaic collectors.

A penthouse mechanical room holds an HRV unit, located in the house's top story to provide cleaner air than would be available at street level and to ensure that the air intake and exhaust ducts to the exterior are kept short. The white acrylic roof is finished with an eco-friendly surfacing material that reflects the sun but does not add contaminates to the rainwater-collection barrels used for irrigating the garden and plants on the roof terrace and in the rear yard.

After a lengthy investigation into the best method to insulate the existing front facade, Fabrica718 decided to apply a layer of exterior insulation and finishing system (EIFS). Because of the extreme temperature differential in New York City, insulating the building from the inside alone can cause a freeze-thaw condition that could harm the masonry wall. (This fear was validated during a winter without occupants—one of the original brick walls cracked because of what looked to be freeze-thaw damage.) The existing brownstone facing would be spalling and degraded. Once construction started, it became

40° 40′

Brooklyn, New York

Fabrica718

2012

Certified by PHI

OPPOSITE: **South-facing facade of the Tighthouse retrofit. The degraded brownstone face veneer was replaced with an EIFS system to provide exterior insulation. The cornice is fiberglass made from a mold of the original. Replacing the original wood cornice allowed for a continuous thermal envelope and air seal at the existing facade.**

evident that it would be better to remove the four-inch face veneer and apply the EIFS, which is similar in appearance to brownstone but more affordable, to the existing masonry. This would not only cut costs but also keep the finish in the same plane with the neighboring building. Most of the three-wythe masonry wall remained in good shape, but areas below the windowsills had to be restored with concrete masonry units (CMU), as the deteriorated stone sills had to be removed. The building's original wood cornice was replaced with a low-maintenance fiberglass replica, which was installed over the EIFS, allowing for a continuous thermal envelope.

On the rear facade, a rainscreen features an air barrier, four inches of rigid mineral wool insulation, and a thermally isolated framing system clad with cement panels, which are durable and low maintenance. Providing both insulation and character to the building, the custom rainscreen panels range in height across the facade to align with window openings and play on typical wood-siding houses often seen in old Brooklyn.

The double-height art studio in the basement consists of a concrete slab that required intricate detailing to meet Passive House standards and satisfy structural and waterproofing requirements. Any penetration through the building's superenvelope could throw off its airtightness, and a failure to stop thermal bridging at the perimeter cellar slab would mean significant heat loss. Fabrica718 collaborated with structural, geotechnical, and Passive House consultant ZeroEnergy Design and decided to line the bottom and the perimeters of the slab with two inches of XPS insulation. A gravel bed and perforated pipe drainage system underneath the slab leads to a sump pump, and a polyethylene membrane just below the slab prevents ground moisture from migrating into the interior space.

Since air sealing of existing stairs can be difficult in retrofit projects, the architects designed new stair openings at each level of the house—the art studio in the basement, a guestroom at the garden level, an open parlor floor for entertaining, a second floor with a home office and children's bedroom, and the master bedroom penthouse and roof terrace. The new staircases allowed the contractor to efficiently air seal the walls before reinstalling the stairs.

In addition, the five sets of stairs became a unifying feature in the house, with their visually exciting but cost-effective design. The plate-steel stringers and perforated stainless-steel treads add special character to the home. The durable and low-maintenance material does not require a finish coat, and the stairs' perforated pattern provides a strong graphic element while bringing natural light to the center of the row house. The stairs are bound by clear glass and, along one wall, a simple handrail that houses LED ribbon lights controlled by eco-timers.

After implementing techniques to maximize daylight at the stairwells, Fabrica718 worked with the clients on a lighting strategy for the rest of the house based on using LED and fluorescent lights limited to five types of fixtures. The challenge was to create gallerylike lighting conditions for the couple's art collection and the studio. The owners eventually opted to install low-cost down lights and track lighting fixtures with the highest-quality retrofit LED bulbs available.

The clients' minimalist aesthetic kept the project unadorned, contributing to the architects' overall goals of energy efficiency and simplicity. Reclaimed materials were used for the industrial flooring on all levels as well as in specific areas of the house, including the parlor space, where a wythe of reclaimed brick was added to coincide with the ceiling opening. This brick was salvaged from the two fireplace flues that were demolished on-site. Custom designs by Brooklyn fabricators include the stainless-steel LED strip lights at the top of each stair landing, which are practical, made locally, and add character to the space.

the architect solved the problem with a triangular-shaped sun sail that is erected during the summer months and retracted for the remainder of the year.

The building's thermal envelope includes the residential entry stair at street level, while the rest of the ground-floor commercial space was not designed to Passive House requirements. The commercial space, a store and showroom that features fashion clothing and objects primarily made from up-cycled materials, includes the storefront and a double-height rear cellar. The interior is of raw concrete and displays the unique markings of the formwork. The proprietor, GGrippo, explains that the combined store and showroom enables him to sell his product line in the store while sharing his creative process with customers in the showroom, as pieces are both designed and assembled there.

In the 174 Grand residence, LoadingDock5 tackled many complicated Passive House detailing issues with inventive solutions. The windows, for example, are at the very surface of the facade, set just inside the front facade's EIFS insulation and lining up with the CMU block behind. The southern rear facade features large windows by the Austrian window manufacturer Walch, selected for their high-efficiency performance and minimalist frame. The panels of fixed glass on the third floor have an area of over six by ten feet; the lower lift-and-slide doors leading out to the deck and garden match them in size but are gasketed and designed to achieve a tight air seal.

The porous CMU sidewalls are painted with white latex paint to achieve airtightness, and ceilings consist of exposed steel panning painted white. A modern floor-to-ceiling glass wall serves as the facade of the commercial space, and in combination with the residence's dark EIFS facade above achieves an interesting graphic effect.

Exciting architectural moments within the house include views of the elevated rear garden, situated above the commercial space below, and of the green roof from various spaces within, as well as open-tread stairs with white zipper stringers that effectively carry light through the building. The top stair flight leads past the master bathroom, allowing visitors a glimpse through its laminated-glass walls just as their own silhouettes become visible from the master bedroom area beyond. These stairs, leading to the green roof, cross the double-height open living space, but because of their light and open design, views of the garden from the master bedroom are still possible.

A critical issue of detailing in an in-fill urban property with neighboring buildings involves exterior insulation at the parapet walls. Early on during the construction, LoadingDock5 discovered that the neighboring structure was leaning into Morath's property by six inches at the top floor and roofline. Negotiations were tricky, but eventually the neighbors agreed to let Morath use exterior insulation along this critical parapet line. The building has seven inches of insulation on the front and rear exteriors and six inches at the side party walls.

While neighboring walls usually help add thermal value to a house, air leaks are a concern, as the shared walls are not necessarily airtight and need to be sealed. To achieve this air seal, LoadingDock5 used latex paint on the CMU block, but blower-door tests still placed the walls out of the required range to achieve Passive House certification. It is hard to determine whether the reason is leakage at the temporary roof hatch or entry door, or whether the latex paint is insufficient. The roof assembly includes ten inches of rigid polyiso insulation and a green roof system with approximately eight inches of soil, which absorbs rainwater runoff while offering visitors a magnificent view of Manhattan.

BELOW: **Green roof with views**
of Manhattan

MORATH ACTED AS the general contractor on this project to control costs, but his combined role as architect/contractor also resulted in innovations.

BELOW: **The rear south-facing facade looks out onto a private elevated deck and garden.**

OPPOSITE: **Open-tread stairs and white zigzag stringers create an open airy stair that carries light throughout the space.**

1 RETAIL
2 BEDROOM
3 MECHANICAL ROOM
4 BATHROOM
5 PLANTER
6 KITCHEN / LIVING / DINING ROOM
7 GREEN ROOF
8 MASTER BEDROOM
9 MASTER BATHROOM
10 TOILET

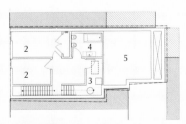

FIFTH FLOOR

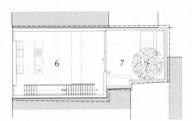

FOURTH FLOOR

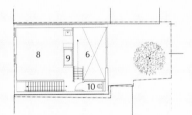

THIRD FLOOR

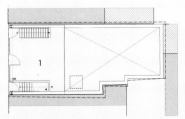

SECOND FLOOR

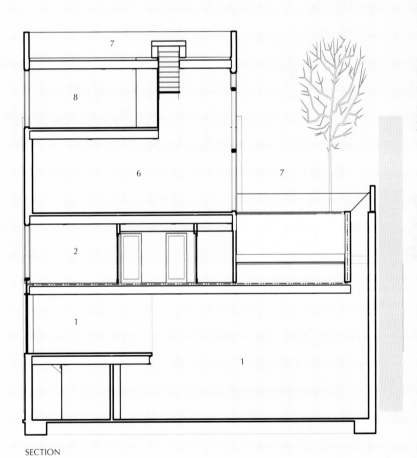

SECTION

ORIENT STUDIO

This Passive House art studio is nestled in coastal scrub brush overlooking the tranquil Long Island Sound. Orient, New York, is at the very tip of the North Fork of Long Island, the low-key, rustic sister to the Hamptons. The small studio is connected to a larger residence on the same property by a gravel pathway flanked with thorny brambles, native black cherry trees, and grapevines. Ryall Porter Sheridan Architects convinced the clients, an artist couple based in New York City, to build their new studio as a Passive House while the firm renovated the existing 1970s home on the property. The architects redesigned the existing residence to stringent Passive House standards, but because it faces north, the project was not able to fully meet Passive House requirements due to the lack of necessary solar heat gain. The new design improves on the home's original architecture with a wide entry ramp that recalls Le Corbusier's Villa Savoye and, in a similar fashion, emphasizes the movement through the house with breathtaking full-height views of the water. While the clients, a video artist, whose studio is in the residence's lower level, and her husband, who paints in the new Passive House studio, are anticipating moving to this quiet hamlet full-time in the future, it currently functions as their second home and studio space.

The Passive House studio building sits on columns and is designed to interfere minimally with the site's natural topography. While grading was required for the new septic tank and for placing the large windows, most foliage and wild growth was undisturbed during construction. The roof features solar photovoltaic panels, and the studio's south-facing facade makes use of an old sustainable concept known as the Trombe wall.

First developed by the French engineer Felix Trombe in the 1960s to allow a house to store and use heat from the sun, Trombe walls usually consist of south-facing stone or brick walls covered with glass, leaving an airflow pathway in between that absorbs solar energy and releases it selectively toward the interior at night. In the art studio building, heat is directed through a cavity in the wall between the CMU and gypsum board that has been left open at the top and bottom to allow air to circulate. Instead of the traditional Trombe-wall glass covering, the architects used a new high-tech material by Sto Corporation, which is used routinely on south-facing walls of warehouses in Germany but is not readily available in the United States. In fact, the manufacturer was hesitant to provide it for this project for fear it would be installed incorrectly. Made up of thousands of plastic fiber strands, the Sto panels capture solar energy and distribute it throughout the interior during the winter months when the sun is low in the sky while blocking out sunlight from higher angles during the summer.

Both the art studio and the nearby home are clad in salvaged Douglas fir joists, which have a beautiful gray patina that blends with the surroundings, and the two buildings feature architect William Ryall's signature screened-in porch that he designed for his own home and several other residences he built in or near Orient. Ryall's own porch sits high above the landscape and encloses a twenty-foot-high space with an open fireplace. This outdoor room is

40° 50′

Orient, New York

Ryall Porter Sheridan Architects

2012

Certified by PHI

OPPOSITE: **View of north elevation of the artist studio with a clerestory for optimized natural-light condition for painting**

safe from the elements but provides fresh air and the sounds of nature. In the artist studio and residence it becomes a clever complement to the Passive House design, which is silent because of the buildings' triple-paned windows and thick airtight blanket envelopes. The thin aluminum surround at exterior windows, seen in both the artist studio and the residence, is another signature detail of the firm. Aluminum is a highly conductive material and would be a linear thermal bridge, but to meet high-energy performance standards Ryall detailed it in a way that leaves it isolated.

For the air seal and weather barriers, the architects used high-performance tape and intelligent membranes. The firm also specified a roof cavity filled with mineral wool insulation as well as dense-packed cellulose for the wall and ceiling insulation. The Pazen-manufactured windows used for both the studio and the home are Passive House–certified and were designed by a German architect with sleek minimalist detailing.

The long clerestory provides coveted northern light to the art studio but required special detailing to achieve the proper insulation at the roofline.

BELOW: **View looking from the house down the ramp to the art studio. Obscured by trees on right is the screened-in porch off of the studio.**

BELOW: The salvaged Douglas fir cladding at the art studio also covers the retrofit home on the property. The reclaimed wood will weather over time.

Sustainable aspects of the interior include the use of reclaimed marble countertops, low-VOC (volatile organic compounds) plywood, and lighting with fluorescent and LED lights.

The substantial retrofit of the residence on the property included thermal insulation and air tightness, Passive House–certified windows, and the installation of an HRV ventilation system. The owners and architect were surprised to find that no insulation was ever installed at the exterior wall cavities of this 1970s home. This energy retrofit project, while not achieving Passive House certification because of gigantic north-facing windows that provide breathtaking views of the coast, is still remarkably energy efficient.

TOP LEFT: **New screened-in porch on the retrofitted home with views of Long Island Sound beyond**

BOTTOM LEFT: **Interior view of the energy retrofit home with views to the water beyond**

TOP RIGHT: **Views of the living area in the retrofit home, which features the same HRV and Passive House–certified windows as the art studio**

BOTTOM RIGHT: **Bathroom of retrofit home with Passive House sliding doors to the roof deck**

OPPOSITE: **Ramped entry to the energy retrofit home**

TOP LEFT: **The Trombe wall at southern elevation of studio. This STO product is used on industrial buildings in Europe and works with plastic rods that carry heat from the sun at specified angles to the interior of the building.**

BOTTOM LEFT: **View of the screened-in porch from the Passive House glass-wall enclosure at the studio**

TOP RIGHT: **Interior view of the art studio. Minimal light fixtures are required at the entry area as natural light filters in through the north-facing clerestory.**

BOTTOM RIGHT: **The corner studio doors by Pazen minimize the frame at the exterior so that doors appear frameless.**

1 STUDIO
2 KITCHENETTE
3 POWDER ROOM
4 COVERED PORCH
5 MAIN HOUSE
6 LONG ISLAND SOUND

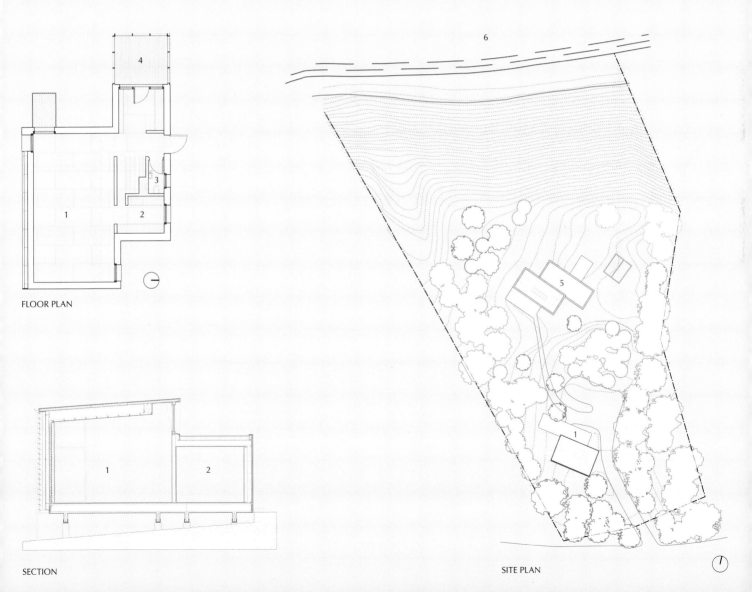

FLOOR PLAN

SECTION

SITE PLAN

WESTPORT HOUSE

The Westport House is a Passive retrofit of a modernist concrete residence built in 1938 a few miles from the Connecticut shoreline. The owner of the home, Doug Mcdonald, is a developer who is profoundly interested in energy-efficient construction and non-toxic building materials. He had previously worked with the architect Ken Levenson on sustainable projects in Brooklyn and commissioned him to help with this tricky Passive House retrofit in 2010.

Mcdonald had originally searched for land in Connecticut that could accommodate a new Passive House structure and make full use of south-facing windows. Not too far into his search he took note of a concrete building with a simple form that had been on the market for several years. The walls revealed evidence of water leakage throughout, but what piqued Mcdonald's interest was that the house was oriented along the property's hillside, instead of facing the street as the vast majority of homes he visited in the area did. He knew that the poured-concrete walls and concrete plank flooring were intrinsically airtight and determined that he could waterproof and repair the concrete surfaces, whose thermal mass would be an asset in achieving an energy-efficient home. With Levenson and the help of PHPP software, Mcdonald realized that the space could be retrofitted as a Passive House. He was so optimistic that he even purchased the high-performance windows for the retrofit weeks before he closed on the home.

To increase the R-value of the walls and roof, Mcdonald and Levenson added FOAMGLAS on the exterior, which could easily be applied to the existing concrete without creating a thermal bridge.

FOAMGLAS is a cellular glass insulation product, made from recycled materials, that performs well in compressive-strength tests and is intrinsically waterproof, vapor tight, and airtight. It is commonly used in Europe to insulate foundation slabs and to create sculptural curves in high-tech architectural buildings. In the United States it has a long history of use on industrial storage tanks but has not often been applied in residences. The material has recently become popular with the Passive House community, but it is still difficult to find craftsmen trained to install it, a common problem with high-performing and cutting-edge materials. Luckily, Mcdonald and Levenson were able to work with FOAMGLAS representatives to learn how to connect gutters and junction boxes to this unconventional material. For his retrofit Mcdonald applied ten inches of FOAMGLAS, which he then covered with a black stucco finish.

The original building featured a signature set of horizontal metal guardrails at each of the three roof terraces that crown the modernist rectangular volumes. To eliminate thermal bridging, Levenson replaced them with CMU blocks, which he insulated thoroughly with FOAMGLAS. To ensure continuity of the thermal envelope, he designed the doors and windows to sit within the FOAMGLAS insulation on pressure-treated wood ledgers. This outbound placement also allows the windows on the south-facing facade to take better advantage of solar heat gain, since there is minimal self-shading from the building. For the roof retrofit, the architect decided on a combination of polyiso and FOAMGLAS.

41° 7'

Westport, Connecticut

Ken Levenson and Douglas Mcdonald

2011

Certified by PHI as EnerPHit

OPPOSITE: **Southeast elevation from the entry driveway. The house is oriented according to the site's landscape and does not face the street as do other neighborhood homes.**

Mcdonald and his family have been living in their Westport home for more than a year and report that it has been a noticeable upgrade in their lives. The house is perfectly quiet at night, and Mcdonald believes that the constant and even flow of ventilated air leaves the members of his family feeling robust and alert when they wake up each morning. Inside the house they can wear short sleeves year round, and the indoor environment, unaffected by drafts and temperature asymmetry, is consistently comfortable. The windows, imported from Optiwin in Germany for their high performance,

open as tilt-and-turns, providing a variety of connections with the outdoors.

Mcdonald expects his home to be operating off the electric grid in another ten years or so. The Westport House already consumes no gas or oil. Solar thermal panels on the roof and a heat pump provide hot water and also feed a small radiant floor system. Rainwater from the property is stored in collection barrels set into an existing planting-bed area. In addition, Mcdonald, who is an innovator at heart, plans to add a filtered-rainwater pool to allow his dogs and children to cool off after a day of playing

BELOW: The original low, modernist window openings were refitted with Passive House–certified windows. Existing fireplaces are difficult to retrofit to Passive House standards. In this case, the owner opted to seal the flue and to use a ventless bioethanol-based fire system in its place.

BELOW: The ten inches of FOAMGLAS insulation added to the exterior of the concrete residence is evident in the depth of the window sills. Frame extensions allow the window to align with the continuous thermal barrier of the FOAMGLAS.

outdoors. The developer is inspired by his reconnection to the countryside after years of living in an urban environment. He firmly believes that humans have moved too far away from living with nature and works to promote and build energy-efficient homes in Connecticut that are made with chemical-free materials.

Meanwhile, Levenson went on to cofound Four Seven Five, a web-based business that sells high-performing building products for Passive House design. Each of the firm's partners has experience working on Passive House projects and understands firsthand that the execution of a Passive House, and particularly of a Passive House retrofit, is difficult if the building products available locally fail to perform as described.

MCDONALD KNEW THAT THE POURED-CONCRETE walls and concrete plank flooring were intrinsically airtight and determined that he could waterproof and repair the concrete surfaces, whose thermal mass would be an asset in achieving an energy-efficient home.

BELOW: Northeast elevation. Rainwater is collected and stored in bins behind the wood fence to the right of the facade to be used later for irrigation on site.

1 KITCHEN / DINING
2 LIVING ROOM
3 POWDER ROOM
4 FAMILY ROOM
5 MUD ROOM
6 BEDROOM
7 STUDY
8 CLOSET
9 BATHROOM
10 MECHANICAL ROOM

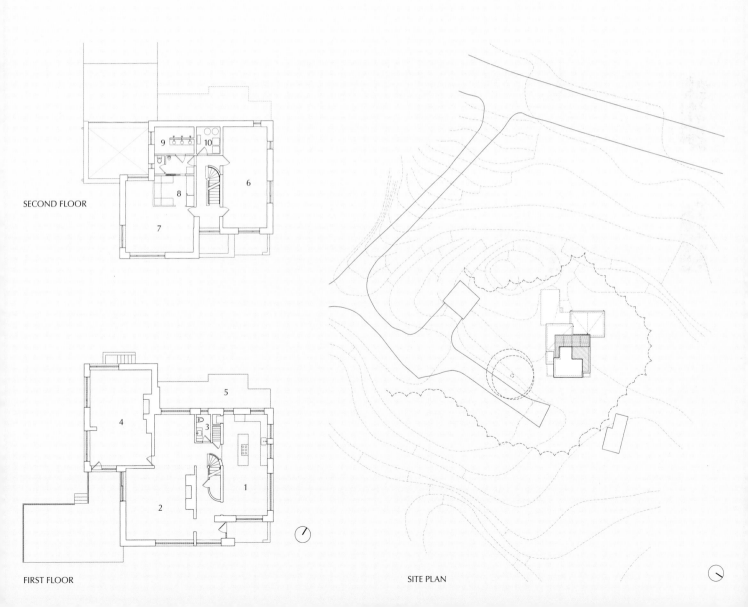

SECOND FLOOR

FIRST FLOOR

SITE PLAN

LITTLE COMPTON

The Little Compton House belongs to a family of six, providing a retreat for a Boston-based couple and their four teenage children. Currently a weekend and summer house, it will likely be the home to which the clients will retire. The house sits on a relatively isolated patch of land in Little Compton, a rural town in southeastern Rhode Island with a population of 3,500. The building is not visible from the street and is surrounded by quiet, pastoral fields. The summer house is just four miles away from the beach and yacht club—an easy bicycle ride for the family.

Boston-based ZeroEnergy Design, a young firm committed to energy efficiency, designed the project. The Little Compton House is the architects' second Passive House project, after a home they designed in Vermont, and is notable for its economical construction. The owners had only a modest budget but were sold on the idea of a modern home that would use 90 percent less heating energy than a typical house. They also had lots of faith in the passionate and talented team they had commissioned. ZeroEnergy Design envisioned a building with a simple, compact shape that was both space and energy efficient. The home's uncomplicated form kept costs fairly low. It is also a play on the traditional gable houses still found in nearby villages and towns. The entry facade faces south with large window apertures. The main feature of the interior is a generous central core that is used as a gathering place. A loft that is accessible by ladder looks out onto the main living space and serves as the children's recreation room and sleeping area. This open layout promotes air circulation, allows for a simplified heating and cooling system, and incorporates a single exposed metal duct passing through the main space.

The master-bedroom suite provides privacy and frames tranquil views of native plantings and wide open fields to the north. Nearby is a room with a large freestanding tub for deep soaking, the owner's one specific luxury requirement. The house's concrete floors are conducive to seaside activities and are complemented by crisp, clean walls and spartan furniture.

To achieve high levels of continuous insulation, the architects bolstered the foundation slab with rigid XPS boards; the double-stud walls contain eleven-inch cavities filled with medium-density spray foam and dense-packed cellulose. The roof, clad with asphalt shingles, is insulated with four-inch XPS at the outermost layer and medium-density spray foam between the trusses. A final blower-door test, done six months after the project was completed, revealed that the air infiltration had increased by about 60 percent over the previous year. The architects' current explanation for the increase is that the water-based medium-density spray foam had shrunk along with the still-drying wood framing. This resulted in connections that became less airtight as both materials pulled away from each other. While this home is still an ultra-low-energy building, ZeroEnergy Design has since modified its detailing to no longer rely on spray foam for its primary air barrier, instead improved taping and sealing tactics and membrane products define the home's primary air barrier.

Although the clients decided to first concentrate on the building's envelope, they will in the near

41° 30'

Little Compton, Rhode Island

ZeroEnergy Design

2011

Not certified

OPPOSITE: Skylights are located near the main entry to maximize natural light in the children's loft and main gathering space.

future install a renewable-energy system. When in place, a mere 4kW photovoltaic system will offset all consumption and allow the project to achieve net zero energy.

BELOW: **Large openings along the southern facade take in solar gain through high-performance windows by Schuco.**

which supplied bath and kitchen fixtures, added luxury to the simple yet high-performing design. The house's HRV system consists of a manifold of supply and extract ventilation ducts that are cleverly hidden from sight.

During the winter months, the house hardly requires heating, as the sun warms the interior through the south-facing facade. The two-foot roof overhang shields against the hottest summer sun, and the low solar heat gain coefficient (SHGC) specified for the glazing prevents excessive solar heat gain during the warmest months. Operable skylights capture

summer breezes, and a wall-mount air-conditioning unit is also readily available (but hardly ever needed). An electric instant tankless water heater provides hot water, and the small amount of supplemental heating needed in the winter is provided through a heat-pump system. There is no gas service to the building. Instead, an induction range and condensing dryer replace typically gas-driven household appliances.

During construction, meticulous site supervision helped the team achieve an airtight building that received an astounding blower-door test result of .149 ACH. When the SIPs, for example, first arrived

BELOW: A few hours of sunlight on a winter day warm up the open living area, which is framed by glue-laminated custom beams supporting the SIP panels overhead.

OPPOSITE: Interior features include a large glass entry door, an open kitchen plan, and a wall-mounted split heat pump—for supplemental heating and cooling—hidden by an angled panel at the center of the loft wall.

on-site, there was an eighth-inch gap between the panels of rigid insulation. To remedy this open seam, holes were drilled in the OSB so that the gaps could be filled with spray foam and resealed. Today DWA's Hudson Passive Project is one of the most energy-efficient homes in the United States and may have broken all records for airtightness.

BELOW: **The open living area and kitchen sit on a concrete floor, which provides thermal mass. The laminated timber beams maximize the building's span, accommodating larger SIP panels with fewer joints.**

1 GREAT ROOM
2 KITCHEN
3 MASTER BEDROOM
4 MASTER BATHROOM
5 BATHROOM
6 STUDY
7 BEDROOM 1
8 BEDROOM 2

BELOW: **Section-diagram detail showing areas requiring special attention to prevent air leakage**

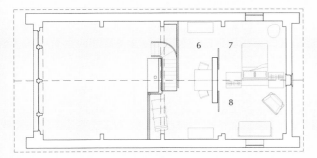

MEZZANINE LOFT

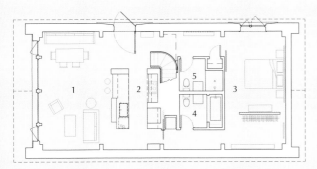

FIRST FLOOR

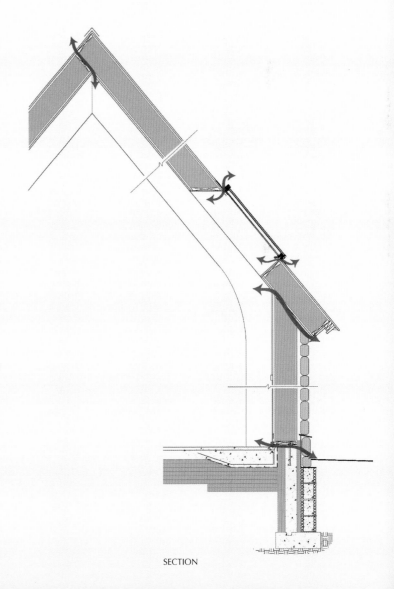

SECTION

R-HOUSE

In 2008 Mark Robbins, former dean at the Syracuse University School of Architecture, and UPSTATE, an interdisciplinary center for design, research, and real estate in the university, sponsored a competition called From the Ground Up, which invited preselected architects to design a model for affordable and sustainable single-family housing for Syracuse's Near Westside neighborhood. The competition was geared at helping revitalize areas within the city that were hard-hit by the economic downturn, such as Near Westside and Southwest, the adjacent neighborhood to the south and one of the poorest in New York State. The university partnered with Home HeadQuarters, a not-for-profit organization that advocates for affordable homes and energy improvement for the underserved, and the Syracuse Center of Excellence to build the three winning homes.

ARO (Architecture Research Office) and Della Valle Bernheimer (now Bernheimer Architecture and Alloy) collaborated on their winning entry. The two firms had previously worked together on a low-income housing project in Brooklyn and were familiar with the conundrum of balancing a budget while providing good and sustainable design. The competition brief was due in early 2008, when the economic downturn had already had an impact on many of New York's architectural offices. ARO's Adam Yarinsky and Andrew Bernheimer joke that there was a "gigantic team" working on the small project during this time because not much other work was happening in the office, as commissions were put on hold or canceled. They embraced the competition

as a challenge that could result in a true paradigm shift in simultaneously meeting the goals of minimal energy consumption, affordability, and innovation for low-income communities. Building these projects would also afford a group of contractors critical training in airtightness and energy efficiency.

At 1,200 square feet, the R-House is roughly the same scale and size of neighboring bungalows but is clad with a corrugated-aluminum finish that is both durable and different and which draws attention to the building. The asymmetrical, angular roof is a play on standard gabled roofs and adds interest to the otherwise simple form. An entry and a rear deck, a nod to the neighboring porch fronts, are cleverly tucked into two diagonally opposite corners of the house, allowing for integral shading and wind protection. This simple way of creating interesting features at the front and back of the building is visually exciting and reflects an understanding of how the house's form relates to the sun's position. The rear facade faces south, and the tall Passive House–certified windows there allow the sun to heat the building during the winter months. To prevent overheating during the summer, the architects planned to add a vine screen to the south facade, but it was never built. The owner eventually added an efficient mini-split air-conditioning system to cool the house.

The team's studies for the interior included plans for flexible layouts to allow the addition of a fourth bedroom when needed. The Lockdeck flooring material specified by the architects is able to span long distances and could easily support an additional bedroom on the second floor. An accessible bedroom

44° 3'

Syracuse, New York

ARO and Della Valle Bernheimer

2010

Certified by PHI

OPPOSITE: A roof overhang at the entry offers the facade of the R-House protection from severe Syracuse weather and is a reinterpretation of Near Westside Syracuse porches. The corrugated-steel panels provide visual interest.

on the first floor can serve as an office or be rented out, providing an opportunity for income. The interior finishes—wood flooring, exposed plywood panels, and a concrete slab that adds thermal mass—are simple and durable and are washed with natural light from the strategically placed windows.

The home's airtight envelope is achieved through wood-truss I-joists and structural panels insulated with dense-packed fiberglass and sheathed with a protective-barrier ZIP system. The foundation slab is insulated with EPS and protected along the perimeter by a frost skirt.

The three winning prototype homes built as a result of the competition are equipped with sensors that monitor energy usage within the residences. A dashboard that displays the current and past energy usage of the R-House is accessible to the public online.

BELOW: **The Near Westside Syracuse neighborhood master plan proposal by ARO and Della Valle Bernheimer, with the paradigm-shifting minimal-energy-consumption prototype houses inserted into vacant lots.**

OPPOSITE: **With its new interpretation of scale and roof line, the R-House aims to spark a dialogue with the neighboring homes visible in the background.**

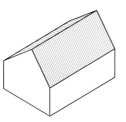 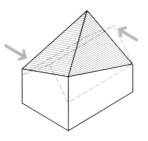 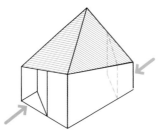

LEFT: Development diagrams

BELOW: **The south facade features large windows for solar heat gain. A foliage screen was planned to protect the windows from overheating in the summer but has yet to be built.**

allowed for a nine-and-a-half-inch-thick layer of dense-packed cellulose and two and a half inches of rigid EPS along the exterior of the walls, behind the rainscreen siding. The EPS insulation continues over the roof, and the I-joist rafter cavities hold almost twelve inches of dense-packed cellulose. In addition to being economical, the I-joist balloon framing allows for a thermal bridge–free connection to the loft floor, as opposed to more common platform framing, which is difficult to insulate at floor-joist connections.

Early in the process, the architects teamed up with a local builder and skilled craftsman to create an airtight thermal envelope. The most challenging area to tape and seal was the connecting vestibule, which required insulating a door with sealers and reinsulating the existing wall. Along the foundation perimeter, an autoclaved aerated concrete (AAC) block creates a thermal break at the wall-to-slab connection. Beneath the concrete floor slab, sixteen inches of EPS insulation protect against heat loss, and a continuous vapor barrier prevents moisture migration from the subsoil.

Unlike most stand-alone Passive House projects, the addition does not include a kitchen, reducing the building's energy loads. Besides a living area, the program included a bedroom as well as open-loft bunk beds for the grandchildren. The entire building is equipped with just four energy-efficient fluorescent light sources. The interior stair is centrally located and features a wood wall that hides high-output fluorescent light fixtures, custom designed by Derrick Porter, along its vertical edge. Light from this source finds its way around the interior by bouncing off white-painted drywall ceilings and perimeter walls. The roof's dramatic angles and the openings between the loft and first floor are used to enliven the space and maximize daylight. The effect is both efficient and exciting, as views and glimpses of spaces beyond beckon visitors as they move through the building.

An ERV provides fresh air ventilation as well as the minimal heating required for the addition. A small, electric baseboard heater in the living room can be used to quickly warm up the space when it has been unoccupied during the winter months.

BriggsKnowles A+D completed the Freeman Passive House in 2010 and are currently studying its energy-usage patterns to size an appropriate wind turbine for the site to achieve net zero energy. The first Passive House designed by the practice has become a benchmark for the partners. As they take on new projects, they are committed to focusing on commissions that employ advanced techniques for energy conservation.

BELOW: **The Passive House addition (right) and the existing building (left)**

BELOW: Made apparent by the lack of a chimney, there is no repetition of a fireplace in the addition, as it would have caused too much heat loss.

THE BOLD, NEW, ULTRAEFFICIENT STRUCTURE, whose walls are twice as thick as the original building's, draws on the sensibility of the old house and local building traditions by maintaining a compact shape with a small surface-to-volume ratio, resulting in minimal exposure to the environment.

LEFT: The addition was designed with just four energy-efficient light fixtures. The custom fixture pictured here was designed by Derrick Porter.

RIGHT: The stair's wooden divider houses thin, high-output fluorescent lights.

LEFT: **First-floor plan, showing the thickness of the Passive House addition's walls**

RIGHT: **The addition's orientation frames views that compliment those of the existing house.**

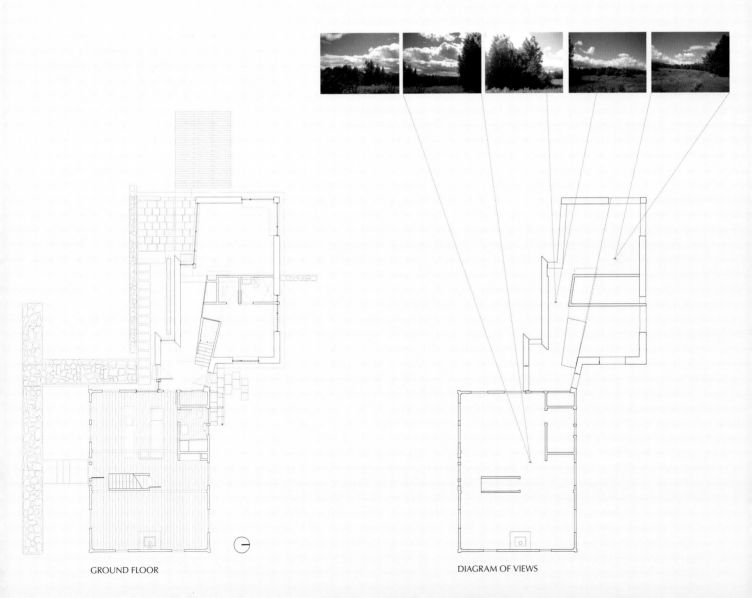

GROUND FLOOR

DIAGRAM OF VIEWS

VOGEL HOUSE

The Vogel House is located on a steep site in a picturesque village at the foothills of the Swiss Alps, a forty-five-minute drive from Zurich, Switzerland's most populous city. The owner, a computer programmer in his forties, had specific wishes for the design that provided programmatic challenges, such as a master bedroom without windows and private outdoor spaces. Diethelm & Spillmann Architekten met, with skilled mastery, the demands posed by the sloped site, local regulations and code constraints, and the client's wish list, creating not only a Passive House but an Energy Plus House that feeds energy back into the grid.

The Zurich-based architects cleverly interpreted the local building code, which does not allow for more than two stories in new construction, in a way that permitted them to define the mezzanine as a roof with deep eaves and skylights. Their main goal was to gain height for the building to provide the client with spectacular views of the Alps and of nearby Lake Aegri. The owner had earlier fixed a camera to a balloon to determine the elevation needed to capture desired views.

The home's footprint on the land is smaller than its overall size, as the first and second floors are cantilevered over the concrete ground-level garage and basement. The elevated residence, with its private vistas through the tree canopy, evokes the dreamlike world of Italo Calvino's *Baron in the Trees* (1957), the story of a young aristocrat who lives in the upper branches of a tree. The plan layout gracefully unfolds around the owner's windowless sleeping chamber and cleverly accommodates both indoor and outdoor private spaces. While a typical Swiss home

incorporates a garden at the ground level, in this case the private garden is elevated and enclosed by walls, with an open roof that accommodates tall vegetation.

The wooden building shell of the first and second floors provides an all-encompassing, warm, interior finish interrupted only by window openings affording spectacular views of the landscape from the living and study areas. The concrete core spaces that include the master and guest bedrooms are finished with refined touches, such as gilded ceilings, and curved corners.

The envelope of the Passive House starts at the concrete slab above the ground floor–level garage and storage room. Exterior stairs lead to a floating patio space with an entry door to the main house. The concrete core structurally supports two large wood beams and dissipates wind loads while also serving as a buffering heat sink. The building easily meets the strict airtightness requirements for Passive House certification, featuring Passive House–certified windows as well as a large wooden entry door that the architects say was the most expensive component of the building envelope. A larch wood blockwall panel system forms the building shell and is designed for high performance. This tight wooden box incorporates two large beams at the upper floor that cantilever fifteen feet above the ground. The beams' depths are enough to accomplish clear spans across the roof, and the resulting cavity was easy to fill with mineral-wool insulation.

Active cooling for residences is not allowed in Switzerland unless there are extraordinary circumstances. The primary means to cool the building in the

47° 4'

Mostelberg, Switzerland

Diethelm & Spillmann Architekten

2010

Certified by Minergie

OPPOSITE: **The cantilevered facade is covered in dark wood cladding with aluminum flakes to reflect the solar radiation and decrease the surface temperature.**

summer is therefore through night cooling, a simple system used in moderate, fairly dry climate zones, such as Central Europe. Windows were placed to maximize local breezes and promote cross ventilation. They are opened at night when the air cools down and closed during the day to retain the cool air. In addition, a so-called earth tube pulls in fresh ventilation through pipes that run in the ground for a set distance before they lead into the HRV. This natural means of cooling the air, used as early as the 1970s, leads to interior temperatures in summer that are about seven degrees cooler than exterior air temperatures.

The roof is covered with solar thermal collectors and solar photovoltaic paneling, providing hot water for domestic use and feeding the hot-air heating system that is sometimes needed during the coldest months. In addition, a small wood-burning stove stores about 80 percent of its energy as hot water. This unit feeds the hot-water tank on cloudy days, providing heat to the system if the solar collectors are not able to generate enough. The solar photovoltaic system provides eight kilowatts per year, exceeding the client's energy consumption. There is no gas service to the building, and most times of the year it

BELOW: The insulated living space maintains a definitive connection with the outdoors, through a wall of windows that frames a view of the Alps in the distance.

TOP LEFT: **The building cantilevers approximately fifteen feet in either direction over the concrete core.**

BOTTOM LEFT: **The Passive House windows in the living area are protected from overheating by a large overhang and the wooden shell that frames the exterior garden.**

RIGHT: **The concrete-block core and panelized-wood exterior shell are highlighted in the entry corridor.**

THEIR MAIN GOAL WAS TO GAIN HEIGHT for the building to provide the client with spectacular views of the Alps and of nearby Lake Aegri. The owner had earlier fixed a camera to a balloon to determine the elevation needed to capture desired views.

feeds energy back into the grid. As Daniel Spillmann stated in an interview with the author, "The goal [for the Vogel House] was not to celebrate the perfect Passive House....On the contrary, it was to prove that even a disadvantageous initial position may lead to a respectable sustainable house." With their design of the Energy Plus home, the architects have certainly done so with great rigor and thoughtfulness.

LEFT: **The private garden is elevated above the entry.**

TOP RIGHT: **The home is located in the foothills of the Swiss Alps, where road conditions make the site difficult to access—so local craftsmen were employed and agricultural tractors were used to deliver materials to the site.**

BOTTOM RIGHT: **The minimalist kitchen includes an angled wall of large windows facing the Alps.**

1 GARAGE
2 MECHANICAL ROOM
3 KITCHEN / LIVING ROOM
4 ELEVATED GARDEN
5 BEDROOM 1
6 BEDROOM 2
7 MASTER BEDROOM
8 OFFICE

BELOW: **Diagram showing the concrete-block core and panelized-wood exterior**

SECOND FLOOR

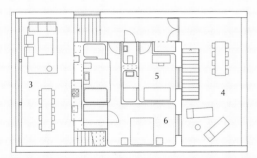

FIRST FLOOR

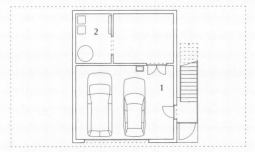

GROUND FLOOR

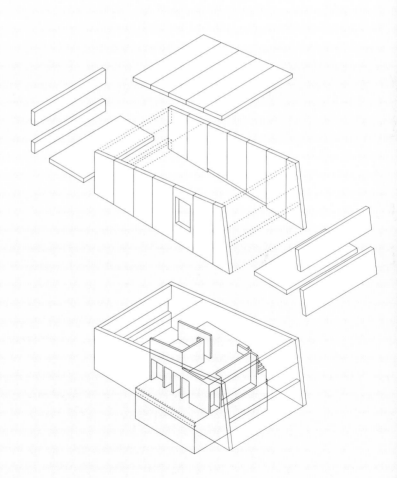

BAMBOO HOUSE

Bessancourt, a sleepy village of 7,400 inhabitants known for its thirteenth-century cathedral, is located eighteen miles northwest of Paris in the Île-de-France region. It is also the setting of France's second Passive House–certified building, the Bamboo House, designed by the Paris-based firm Karawitz Architecture. The simple form of the single-family residence was partly a result of local urban-planning regulations. Fortunately, a compact shape is also an advantage in Passive House design.

The entire house, including the roof, is clad with a grid of bamboo poles that give the simple form a sculptural feel. The natural material is left unfinished and, at the exterior, will weather over time. The unconventional use of bamboo adds visual interest to the compact dwelling, which is mostly opaque on the north facade while open along the southern face with large areas of glazing for solar gain. No cooling is required in this north-central region of France, so the primary use of energy is for heating. Metal-grille balconies on the south facade support a moveable bamboo screen system that can be arranged in various ways to prevent overheating in summer. During July and August, when the sun is highest and strongest, the screens can be closed completely to shade the metal balconies while allowing natural light into the interior spaces, providing ever-changing effects for the residents as light passes through the screens during the day. In winter, with the screens left open, the only supplemental heating comes from radiators in each of the two bathrooms, but they are rarely used.

Both the house's site orientation and plan organization follow Passive House principles but are exceptionally eloquent and unique in their execution. The plan is arranged around a central service spine designed with wood fins spaced at regular intervals across the length of the house. Providing ventilation, electrical, and lighting services for the home, this area is easily accessible to residents and playfully reveals the house's inner workings. Sanitary and circulation spaces are to the north of this spine, with living and sleeping quarters along the house's southern end, in a one-to-two proportion. The interior spaces are small but lively, with warm natural-wood walls and ceilings.

The building's thermal envelope consists of cross-laminated timber I-joists with dense-packed cellulose and wood-fiber insulating board. The foundation slab is of screed concrete with rigid insulation below. The sloped roof features solar thermal panels, which provide most of the hot water for the home, and solar photovoltaic panels, which capture enough solar energy to earn this building an Energy Plus rating in France. For cloudy days, a heat pump is available.

The Bamboo House, the architects' own home, is a showcase for describing the couple's green vision, and they have hosted many clients and visitors who are curious about Passive House design. With the success of this award-winning project, which was completed in January 2009, Karawitz Architecture can today boast a current project list that is made up of more than 75 percent Passive Houses. The firm also recently completed a Passive House–certified retrofit.

49° 2'

Bessancourt, France

Karawitz Architecture

2009

Certified by PHI

OPPOSITE: **Bamboo suncreens provide privacy to the residents of this Passive House while also creating a dynamic play of light and shadow on the exterior, especially during the evening.**

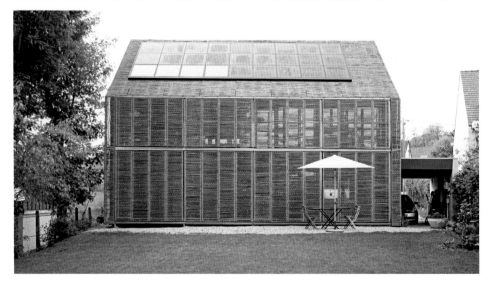

LEFT: The adjustable sunscreens create an ever-changing sculptural form in the landscape.

BELOW: **The thermal mass of the concrete floor retains warmth from solar gains.**

THE SIMPLE FORM of the single-family residence was partly a result of local urban-planning regulations. Fortunately, a compact shape is also an advantage in Passive House design.

OPPOSITE: **The metal-grille system that supports the sunscreens creates additional habitable exterior space.**

TOP LEFT: **The kitchen range has a recirculating fan and a separate ventilation exhaust to remove odors and excess humidity. A direct-vent exhaust hood is not advisable in Passive House construction since it combats airtightness.**

BOTTOM LEFT: **Operable high-performance doors allow the owner to access the metal-grille balcony.**

RIGHT: **The nursery features simple, unfinished, and natural wood surfaces.**

LEFT: **The bathrooms feature natural-wood finishes and backup radiant heating.**

RIGHT: **Central wood fins are located at regular intervals, defining a semiprivate play area while also carrying building services.**

1 MECHANICAL ROOM
2 POWDER ROOM
3 KITCHEN / DINING
4 LIVING ROOM
5 STUDY
6 OFFICE

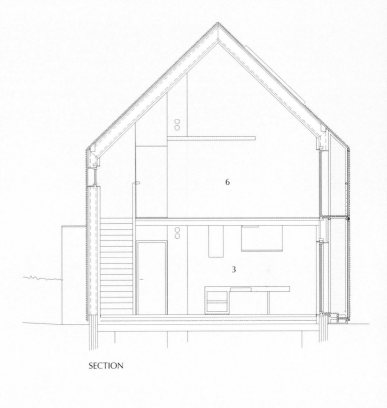

SECTION

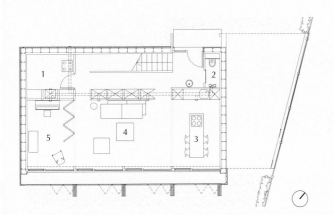

FIRST FLOOR

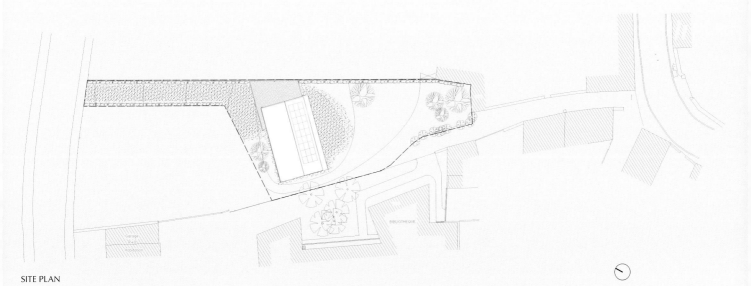

SITE PLAN

AUSTRIA HOUSE

The Austrian Passive House Group (APG), which consists of five Austrian companies working in energy-efficient construction and Passive House design, built the 2,700-square-foot Austria House for the 2010 Olympic Winter Games in Whistler, Canada, in an effort to share Passive House technology with Canada and the entire Olympic community. Designed by Vienna's Treberspurg & Partner Architekten, the Austria House is the first Passive House–certified building in Canada and one of the most energy-efficient structures ever built for the Olympic Games. The international aspect of the collaboration took more time to develop than did the actual construction, which occurred during the fall of 2009. The quick and flawless process was a great marketing opportunity for Austria and highlighted the country's high-performance-manufacturing capabilities.

The house's compact structure and gabled roof recall traditional Alpine ski lodges. Large areas of glazing, consisting of Passive House–certified windows, and an outdoor terrace and plaza on the south, provide views of the Blackcomb and Whistler Mountains, where the Olympic events were held. The panelized wall-and-roof system, with solid tongue-and-groove oak strips, resulted in an interior that is visually warm and inviting as well as efficiently constructed. There was no need for gypsum board and plastered finishes, as the SIPs themselves are finished, airtight interior cladding. The shingled cement board on the exterior adds a friendly scale and texture to the otherwise austere building. Along the house's eastern side, at the outdoor balcony, a profile of the roofline reveals the thickness of the

insulation assembly—the only visible indication that this is a Passive House.

During the Olympic events, the Austria House hosted a television crew and the Austrian Olympic judges. The building's lower floor was designed for public use and contained a small café area; festivities with food vendors were staged on the plaza in front of the building. The lounge areas on the upper level can be reached via both interior and exterior stairs. According to Matheo Durfeld, the Canadian contractor in charge of the construction site, the building performed well for the events it hosted, although the windows of the small house, a space designed for low occupancy, had to be opened to prevent over-heating on the few occasions when there were large gatherings.

Every component of the building, including the stairs and deck, was engineered and built in the Sohm Holzbautechnik factory in Austria. The prefabricated elements arrived in five shipping containers and were assembled on-site within a month. The building's wall-and-roofing panels are unique because of their solid, tongue-and-groove, four-inch-thick interior wood mass. While gaskets and tapes are required to aid in air sealing along seams, the wood-doweled product requires no metal fasteners or glue to be secured in place. This top-of-the-line Austrian product, designed specifically for the cold Whistler climate, was factory-filled with more than twelve inches of fiberglass-batt insulation and at the roof with more than seventeen inches of insulation. Because of shipping logistics, some of the fiberglass-batt insulation was installed on-site. The building's foundation is made of IsoQuick,

50° 7'

Whistler, Canada

Treberspurg & Partner Architekten

2010

Certified by PHI

OPPOSITE: **The Austria House's large south-facing windows on the ground floor highlight the building's public nature.**

an insulated system segmented into small blocks that snap together like the pieces of a LEGO set, allowing the foundation to be tightly insulated from the ground.

The building site was designed to accommodate a horizontal field for a ground-source heat-pump system that provides supplemental heat and hot-water services and feeds into a compact HRV system. This type of HRV system is frequently referred to as a "magic box" because of its simplicity, compactness, and ability to support plug-in solutions for heat, water, and energy-supply systems, including solar thermal energy.

After the Olympic Games, the management of the building was handed over to the municipality of Whistler. Located about 150 miles northeast of Vancouver, the small town is a hub of skiing, hiking, and other outdoor activities. Tourism is an important component of the town's economy, and the Austria House is a showcase building that today houses the Nordic Ski Club and the Whistler Off-Road Cycling Association. A website for the project continues to feature a live feed of the building's energy usage. Thus far, the only type of maintenance that the building has required is the regular replacement of the HRV air filter.

BELOW: **Cement-fiber shingles cover the facade and roof.**

The Rainbow Duplex is part of Whistler's initiative to create affordable housing for a more diversified workforce in an area best known for tourism and outdoor recreation. The municipality is determined to support future Passive House and other low-energy projects, a pledge local authorities made in the Whistler 2020 Sustainable Vision. A trip by the heads of Whistler's building and planning departments to Austria on the invitation of the Austrian Passive House Group, along with the success of the Austria House, played a big role in educating local leaders in Passive House technology and helped bring the project to fruition.

BELOW: **View of the rear facade with the Blackcomb Mountains beyond. The single mini-split condensers used for supplemental heating in each unit are mounted above the snow line.**

BELOW: Each Rainbow Duplex unit has a two-story living space that contains the Passive House envelope. The concrete garage and storage unit are outside this envelope.

THE RAINBOW DUPLEX is part of Whistler's initiative to create affordable housing for a more diversified workforce in an area best known for tourism and outdoor recreation.

LEFT: View showing automated external blinds in various positions to block out sun during certain times of day and prevent overheating

RIGHT: Detail of Optiwin triple-paned window with thermal bridge–free frame and recessed box-frame system with rigid insulation to further limit conduction points

1 BEDROOM
2 BATHROOM
3 COFFEE AREA
4 OFFICE
5 CLOSET

SECOND FLOOR

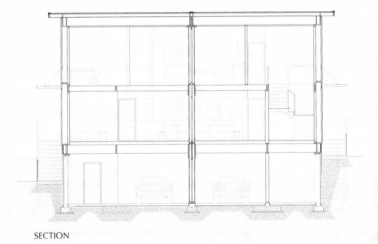

SECTION

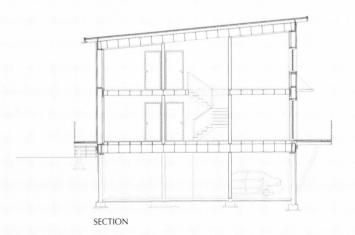

SECTION

TEXTILE HOUSE

The Textile House, completed in 2008, is a detached Passive House in Asse, Belgium, on the outskirts of Brussels. Because of the sloping site, the house sits on two levels, with the first floor, which contains private bedrooms at the back and a home office facing the street, partly underground. Calling the need for enclosed private property into question, BLAF Architecten added a public front-yard basketball court on the leveled portion of the property that invites the neighborhood to play.

The first-floor facade fronting the basketball court has an ethylene propylene diene monomer rubber (EPDM) surface, creating a canvas for chalkboard artists and neighborhood children. As Lieven Nijs, a partner at BLAF Architecten, explains, the material was an economical way to avoid thermal bridging at the facade, because it is light and thin and adheres easily without fasteners to the exterior insulation. The chalkboard concept evolved accidentally one day when the owner, an architect at BLAF Architecten, used the facade to leave a message, writing "I'll be back in five minutes" on the rubber surface. Soon, neighborhood children and artist friends, including Belgian artist Eva Mouton, began to draw on the walls.

The lower level of the house, composed mainly of poured concrete and masonry blocks with XPS insulation, is buried into the hillside, and its thermal mass retains both heat and cold. The upper story is clad in a UV-resistant glass-fiber fabric, resulting in a facade made up entirely of sunshades, automated at window areas and otherwise fixed on wooden frames. Part of the architects' decision to limit the exterior cladding to the glass-fiber fabric that gave the project its moniker, Textile House, was to avoid the blatant material dissonance between the moveable shading device and the building facade. Behind the textile panels is a masonry and timber-frame wall filled with dense-packed cellulose insulation; the roof employs a tapered rigid insulation.

The interior plan layout is unusual in that the private spaces are on the darker, massive lower level, while the living room and kitchen are on the upper level, overlooking the basketball court with lots of windows and natural light. In addition to the operable sunscreen shades at the upper-level windows, golden curtains are strategically located to easily close off portions of the full-height glass facade for more privacy. A skylight and open-stair core bring light into the center of the home. The custom-designed stair includes built-in seating benches at the bottom that lend themselves to entertainment or play areas.

The residence is outfitted with a Magic Box that provides ventilated air through an HRV and hot water via a heat pump. There is no gas service to the building, and a rainwater-collection tank in the front yard provides water for the toilets and irrigation. BLAF Architecten designed the home to be an Energy Plus House. In addition to meeting Passive House standards, the house is outfitted with twenty solar photovoltaic panels that generate an excess of 6302 kWh, which is fed back into the power grid. While solar panels are most effective after a building's energy consumption has already been greatly reduced through other sustainable practices (and the Passive House standard does not list solar photovoltaic

50° 54′

Asse, Belgium

BLAF Architecten

2008

Certified by the Flemish Passive House Platform

OPPOSITE: **Temporary wall art by the Belgian artist Eva Mouton**

power as part of the certification criteria), the Belgian government, in an effort to reduce CO_2 emissions and to comply with the Kyoto Protocol, has created a program that offers large subsidies to home owners who add solar panels to their houses. The paradoxical outcome of this well-intentioned government program is that the cost of electricity has actually increased in Belgium, since power distribution companies must write checks to home owners who feed the grid.

With their Textile House and other recent Passive House projects, BLAF Architecten are a key part of the recent push for sustainability in and around Brussels, which has achieved more than 2,500,000 square feet of Passive House construction in only four years, well ahead of the goals set by the EU Performance in Building Directive.[1]

1   Wolfgang Feist, "Press Release for the 4 May 2012 Press Conference on the 16th International Passive House Conference 2012, Conference Master Plan for the European Energy Revolution," May 9, 2012, www.passivehouseconference.org.

BELOW: **The rear facade features a private wood deck, and the lower level of the house is nestled into the land.**

RIGHT: The upper level of the facade is formed by wood-frame panels that hold fiber-fabric panels, and the lower level has rubber roofing material used as cladding.

TOP: **High-performance glazing brings in natural light from the front and rear facades.**

BOTTOM: **Interior curtains provide privacy in the very open house, where light fixtures are minimized because daylight has been maximized.**

RIGHT: **The central stair is a gathering space and brings natural light down to the ground floor, which is partly bermed.**

OPPOSITE: **Larger corner windows are set with an overhang to hide the operable shading device and avoid overheating in summer.**

THE CHALKBOARD CONCEPT evolved accidentally one day when the owner, an architect at BLAF Architecten, used the facade to leave a message, writing *"I'll be back in five minutes"* on the rubber surface. Soon, neighborhood children and artist friends began to draw on the walls.

LEFT: Glass in the building's core helps carry natural light into all areas of the home.

RIGHT: Gathering spaces, such as the open kitchen and dining area, are located along the front facade, allowing for direct interplay with the neighborhood.

1 MASTER BEDROOM
2 TECHNICAL ROOM
3 STORAGE ROOM
4 MASTER BEDROOM
5 ENTRANCE
6 OFFICE
7 SPARE BEDROOM

8 CHILDREN'S AREA
9 CHILDREN'S BATHROOM
10 CHILDREN'S BEDROOM
11 LIVING ROOM
12 DINING ROOM
13 KITCHEN
14 TERRACE

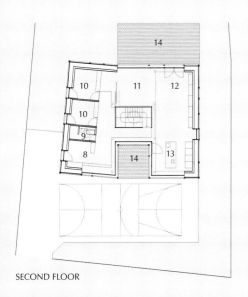

SECOND FLOOR

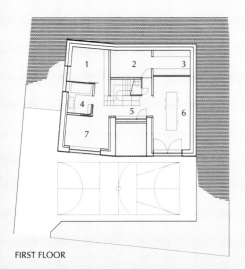

FIRST FLOOR

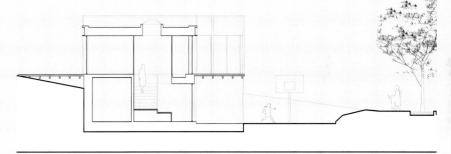

SECTION

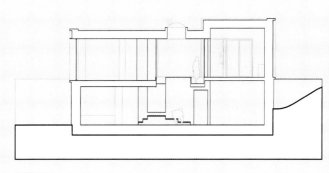

SECTION

CARRAIG RIDGE PROJECT

Seattle-based Olson Kundig Architects, a firm known for its emphasis on craft and buildings that connect to their natural surroundings, designed the Carraig Ridge Project prototype, a residence intended for a three-hundred-year building life cycle, with both the poetics of architecture and high performance in mind. The criteria for design included durability, extreme energy efficiency, adaptability, and delight. The model house is part of a master plan of nine units, which will be grouped together on an overwhelmingly beautiful natural site, located an hour's drive outside of Calgary, Alberta. Each unit will occupy less than five acres to minimize disturbance to the land and maximize views, and each building is set to gently straddle the natural border between the landscape's aspen forest and open prairie. To reduce the project's impact on the land, which is next to a four-thousand-acre nature preserve, the architects decided to use prefabricated module parts that allow for fast construction and can be later disassembled for recycling.

The Carraig Ridge prototype, consisting of a main house, a central exterior deck, and a separate guesthouse, sits on a long, concrete, rectangular platform supported by three concrete piers. The approach is via a wooden walkway that cuts through the forest to the concrete platform. The main house is on level with the aspen tree canopy and the guesthouse at the opposite end of the concrete pad floats over the prairie. A utility chase runs beneath the concrete-plank slabs, permitting services to be shared between the main house and guesthouse, and can easily be accessed through cavities in the three piers.

The house, which is designed to meet stringent Passive House standards, is clad with thermally isolated steel sections and features large areas of high-performance triple-glazed insulated glass units (IGUs), which are imported from Germany. The architects thoroughly researched site orientation, thermal insulation, and window sizes to achieve a highly optimized facade system that balances thermal resistance, solar heat gain, and the desire for large glass areas. The use of high R-value windows will result in a glass facade that is comfortable to stand next to and touch even in winter, allowing residents to be engaged with and connected to the environment in a new and more intimate way. Analysis of sun angles during every season informed the roof overhang as well as the motorized floor-mounted external shading devices that prevent low sun from entering and overheating the interior. External attenuated-steel columns support the high end of the steel roof and allow for expansive and uninterrupted views of the landscape.

The prototype's orientation on the site provides optimal views without significantly increasing energy usage, thus achieving a perfect balance between outdoor vistas and solar gain while eliminating the possibility of overheating. Analysis of the prevailing wind, which fluctuates in intensity and direction depending on the season, was another important consideration when siting the building.

The smart envelope allows for a lean mechanical system. In the Carraig Ridge model house, a horizontal field loop for a ground-source heat-pump system provides heat in winter and extracts heat from the building in summer while supplying hot water

51° 3'

Ghost Lake, Canada

Olson Kundig Architects

Prototype Design Spring 2012

OPPOSITE: **Attenuated columns on the large spans of frameless glass allow for maximized landscape views.**

to the building throughout the year. The heat transfer efficiency gained from the constant ground temperature makes the ground-source heat pump more
efficient than an air-source heat pump, although it is
more expensive to install. Even though Olson Kundig
Architects determined that the home will perform
with less than 90 percent of the energy required to
operate the average Canadian residence, the designers added solar photovoltaic panels to bring the project to net zero. The one-thousand-square-foot home
will only require only a 1.9 kWh solar array to cover
the estimated annual energy use of 2,497 kWh.

BELOW: **Three simple piers
anchor the platform and limit
disturbance to the landscape at
ground level.**

BELOW: **The guest house is located on same platform as the main house and linked by an exterior deck.**

TO REDUCE THE PROJECT'S IMPACT on the land, which is next to a four-thousand-acre nature preserve, the architects decided to use prefabricated module parts that allow for fast construction and can be later disassembled for recycling.

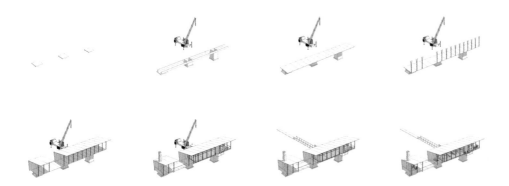

TOP: **Diagram showing the prefabricated, modular construction enabling easy assembly and disassembly**

MIDDLE: **The four-thousand-acre nature preserve consists of two distinct landscapes: open prairie and aspen forest.**

BOTTOM: **Rendering illustrating the outward orientation of the house, which attempts to rest on its site as lightly as possible**

1 ENTRY BRIDGE
2 ENTRY VESTIBULE
3 LIVING ROOM
4 DINING ROOM
5 KITCHEN
6 BEDROOM
7 LADDER TO LOFT
8 RAISED PLATFORM
9 DECK

SITE PLAN

MAIN LEVEL

KAMAKURA

Key Architects

OPPOSITE: Blower-door test in process. Also shown here are the intelligent membrane, air barrier tape, and furring strips for the service cavity.

Project location	Kamakura, Japan
Climate zone	humid subtropical
Heating degree days	2695°F·days/yr (1497 K·days/yr)
Cooling degree days	518°F·days/yr (288 K·days/yr)
Treated-floor area	840 ft² (78 m²)
Airtightness	0.14 ACH at 50 Pa
Number of blower-door tests	1
Primary energy demand	35.8 kbtu/ft²·yr (113 kWh/m²·yr)
Wall R-value and U-value	R-35.5, U=0.028 btu/ft²·hr·°F (0.16W/m²·K)
Roof R-value and U-value	R-25.8, U=0.039 btu/ft²·hr·°F (0.22W/m²·K)
Floor R-value and U-value	R-56.8, U=0.018 btu/ft²·hr·°F (0.1W/m²·K)
Window U-value (installed)	0.15 btu/ft²·hr·°F (0.85W/m²·K)
Space-heating demand	4.75 kbtu/ft²·yr (15 kWh/m²·yr)
Space-cooling demand	4.75 kbtu/ft²·yr (15 kWh/m²·yr)
Heating-equipment type	air-source heat pump
Heating-equipment efficiency	20.5 HSPF; 6.0 COP
Cooling-equipment type	air-source heat pump
Cooling-equipment efficiency	20.5 HSPF; 6.0 COP
Hot-water-equipment type	heat pump hot water
Hot-water-equipment efficiency	3.2 Energy Factor; 3.2 COP
Ventilation-system type	HRV
Ventilation-system efficiency	90%
Renewable-energy systems	none

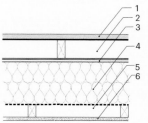

ROOF R-25.8
1 wood deck with vent cavity below
2 metal roofing
3 structural board, 24 mm
4 timber beam, 500 mm with wood-fiber insulation
5 moisture adaptive barrier with service cavity 100 mm
6 plaster board 12.5 mm

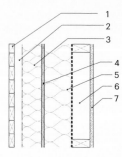

WALL R-35.5

1 wood cladding, 11 cm
2 vent cavity, 18 mm
3 100 mm wood fiber
4 9 mm structural board
5 moisture adaptive vapor barrier
6 timber stud with 144 mm wood fiber
7 service cavity with moisture adaptive vapor barrier, 30 mm

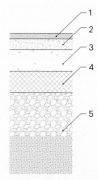

SLAB R-56.8

1 1-in timber wood flooring
2 2-in screed
3 4-in concrete slab
4 100 mm XPS
5 ground

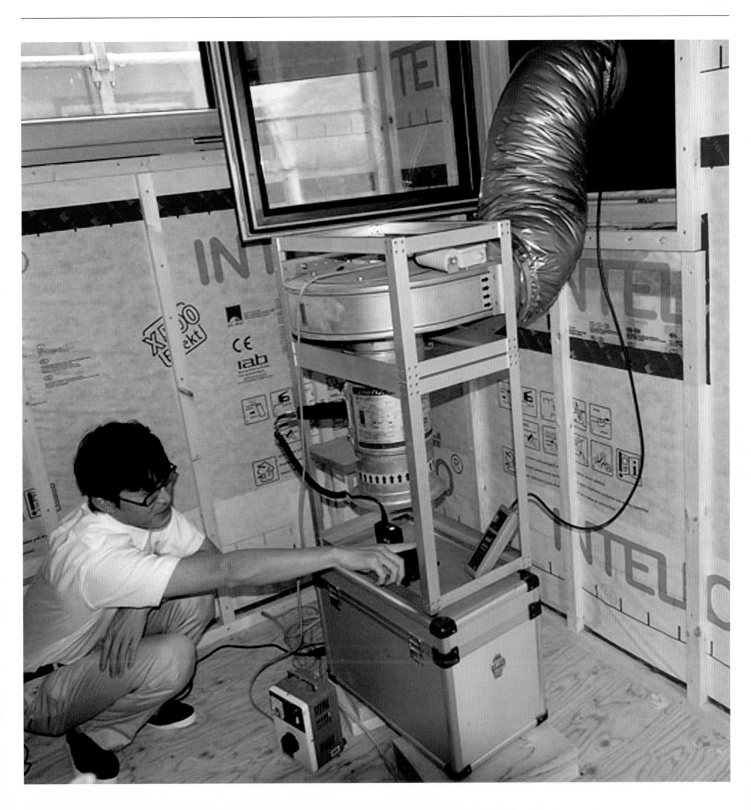

PRESCOTT HOUSE

Studio 804

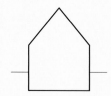

OPPOSITE: Students in Studio 804 hoist the TJI-framed wall assembly into place.

Project location	Kansas City, KS
Climate zone	mixed humid
Heating degree days	5500°F·days/yr (3056 K·days/yr)
Cooling degree days	1300°F·days/yr (722 K·days/yr)
Treated-floor area	1725 ft² (160 m²)
Airtightness	0.54 ACH at 50 Pa
Number of blower-door tests	3
Primary energy demand	36.7 kbtu/ft²·yr (115.8 kWh/m²·yr)
Wall R-value and U-value	R-53, U=0.019 btu/ft²·hr·°F (0.107W/m²·K)
Roof R-value and U-value	R-47.2, U=0.021 btu/ft²·hr·°F (0.120W/m²·K)
Floor R-value and U-value	R-78.6, U=0.013 btu/ft²·hr·°F (0.072W/m²·K)
Window U-value (installed)	U=0.17 btu/ft²·hr·°F (0.965W/m²·K)
Space-heating demand	4.12 kbtu/ft²·yr (13 kWh/m²·yr)
Space-cooling demand	1.06 kbtu/ft²·yr (3.3 kWh/m²·yr)
Heating-equipment type	air-source heat pump
Heating-equipment efficiency	10.1 HSPF; 2.96 COP
Cooling-equipment type	air-source heat pump
Cooling-equipment efficiency	17 HSPF; 4.98 COP
Hot-water-equipment type	electric
Hot-water-equipment efficiency	0.95 Energy Factor; 0.95 COP
Ventilation-system type	ERV
Ventilation-system efficiency	77%
Renewable-energy systems	none

ROOF R-47.2

1 4-in polyiso beneath 25-gauge galvalume roofing
2 16-in engineered-wood I-joist with cellulose
3 5/8-in gypsum white board (GWB)

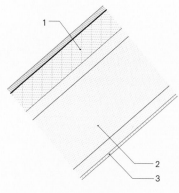

WALL R-53

1 Douglas fir side with 1/4-in spacing
2 air cavity
3 3-in EPS
4 1/2-in plywood
5 12-in engineered wood I-joist with cellulose
6 1/2-in GWB

SLAB R-78.6

1 4-in slab
2 9-in EPS
3 compacted rock fill

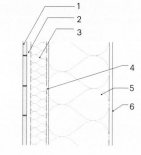
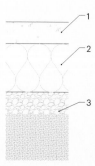

TWO POINT FIVE

ISA and Postgreen

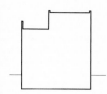

OPPOSITE: SIP wall panels being stacked and readied for installation at the 100k House

Project location	Philadelphia, PA
Climate zone	mixed humid
Heating degree days	5055°F·days/yr (2808 K·days/yr)
Cooling degree days	1476°F·days/yr (820 K·days/yr)
Treated-floor area	1629 ft² (151 m²)
Airtightness	0.55 ACH at 50 Pa
Number of blower-door tests	1
Primary energy demand	31.0 kbtu/ft²·yr (97.8 kWh/m²·yr)
Wall R-value and U-value	R-40, U=0.025 btu/ft²·hr·°F (0.142W/m²·K)
Roof R-value and U-value	R-46, U=0.022 btu/ft²·hr·°F (0.123W/m²·K)
Floor R-value and U-value	R-51.8, U=0.019 btu/ft²·hr·°F (0.110W/m²·K)
Window U-value (installed)	0.23 btu/ft²·hr·°F (1.306W/m²·K)
Space-heating demand	7.85 kbtu/ft²·yr (24.8 kWh/m²·yr)
Space-cooling demand	1.55 kbtu/ft²·yr (4.9 kWh/m²·yr)
Heating-equipment type	air-source heat pump
Heating-equipment efficiency	10.0 HSPF; 2.93 COP
Cooling-equipment type	air-source heat pump
Cooling-equipment efficiency	17.0 HSPF; 4.98 COP
Hot-water-equipment type	SHW with electric backup
Hot-water-equipment efficiency	0.92 Energy Factor; 0.92 COP
Ventilation-system type	ERV
Ventilation-system efficiency	81%
Renewable-energy systems	2kW PV; solar hot water

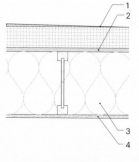

ROOF R-46

1 rigid insulation with waterproofing membrane
2 plywood
3 TJI roof/ceiling construction with cellulose
4 5/8-in GWB

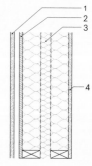

WALL R-40

1 fiber cement on furring strips
2 sheathing with integral weather barrier
3 9-in double-stud framing with cellulose
4 5/8-in GWB

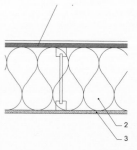

FIRST FLOOR R-51.8

1 plywood subfloor
2 14-in TJI floor construction with cellulose insulation
3 5/8-in GWB

BELFIELD

Onion Flats

OPPOSITE: The Zip system, with tape at all joints and around all windows, is visible on prefabricated modules in the factory prior to on-site construction.

Project location	Philadelphia, PA
Climate zone	mixed humid
Heating degree days	5475˚F·days/yr (3042 K·days/yr)
Cooling degree days	1476˚F·days/yr (820 K·days/yr)
Treated-floor area	4443 ft² (413 m²)
Airtightness	0.40 ACH at 50 Pa
Number of blower-door tests	1
Primary energy demand	34.9 kbtu/ft²·yr (110.1 kWh/m²·yr)
Wall R-value and U-value	R-33.5, U = 0.030 btu/ft²·hr·˚F (0.170W/m²·K)
Roof R-value and U-value	R-52, U = 0.019 btu/ft²·hr·˚F (0.109W/m²·K)
Floor R-value and U-value	R-56.8, U = 0.018 btu/ft²·hr·˚F (0.100W/m²·K)
Window U-value (installed)	0.15 btu/ft²·hr·˚F (0.83W/m²·K)
Space-heating demand	4.43 kbtu/ft²·yr (14.0 kWh/m²·yr)
Space-cooling demand	4.12 kbtu/ft²·yr (13.0 kWh/m²·yr)
Heating-equipment type	air-source heat pump
Heating-equipment efficiency	11.6 HSPF; 3.40 COP
Cooling-equipment type	air-source heat pump
Cooling-equipment efficiency	11.6 HSPF; 3.40 COP
Hot-water-equipment type	heat pump
Hot-water-equipment efficiency	2.35 Energy Factor; 2.35 COP
Ventilation-system type	ERV
Ventilation-system efficiency	84%
Renewable-energy systems	5kW PV

ROOF R-52

1 EPDM roofing membrane
2 polyisocyanurate tapered insulation
3 2-in polyisocyanurate rigid insulation
4 3/4-in tongue and groove (T&G) fire retardant plywood
5 dense-packed cellulose insulation
6 5/8-in GWB

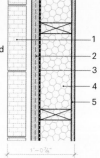

WALL R-33.5

1 brick veneer
2 two layers of 1-in foil-faced polyisocyanurate rigid-board insulation joints staggered and taped
3 wall sheathing with integral air and moisture barrier
4 2x6 wood studs with dense-packed cellulose insulation
5 GWB

SLAB R-56.8

1 dense-packed cellulose insulation
2 sheathing with integral air and moisture barrier
3 rigid insulation
4 gravel

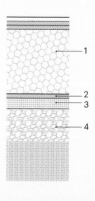

TIGHTHOUSE

Fabrica718

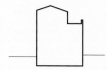

OPPOSITE:
TOP LEFT: EPS rigid-foam board is a component of the STO EIFS system on the building's front facade.
TOP RIGHT: A Solitex membrane forms the connection between the new penthouse walls and roof, assuring a continuous air barrier.
BOTTOM LEFT: A continuous fifteen-mil polyethylene sheet underneath the new concrete slab
BOTTOM RIGHT: Perforated piping and sloped gravel underneath the cellar slab provide drainage.

Project location	Brooklyn, NY
Climate zone	mixed humid
Heating degree days	5000°F·days/yr (2778 K·days/yr)
Cooling degree days	1050°F·days/yr (583 K·days/yr)
Treated-floor area	2203 ft² (205 m²)
Airtightness	0.38 ACH at 50 Pa
Number of blower-door tests	5
Primary energy demand	35.2 kbtu/ft²·yr (111.1 kWh/m²·yr)
Wall R-value and U-value	R-30.4, U=0.033 btu/ft²·hr·°F (0.187W/m²·K)
Roof R-value and U-value	R-55.7, U=0.018 btu/ft²·hr·°F (0.102W/m²·K)
Floor R-value and U-value	R-11.2, U=0.089 btu/ft²·hr·°F (0.507W/m²·K)
Window U-value (installed)	0.17 btu/ft²·hr·°F (0.965W/m²·K)
Space-heating demand	4.63 kbtu/ft²·yr (14.6 kWh/m²·yr)
Space-cooling demand	1.42 kbtu/ft²·yr (4.5 kWh/m²·yr)
Heating-equipment type	air-source heat pump
Heating-equipment efficiency	9.0 HSPF; 2.64 COP
Cooling-equipment type	air-source heat pump
Cooling-equipment efficiency	15 HSPF; 4.40 COP
Hot-water-equipment type	heat pump
Hot-water-equipment efficiency	0.92 Energy Factor; 0.92 COP
Ventilation-system type	HRV
Ventilation-system efficiency	84%
Renewable-energy systems	2.5kW PV

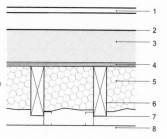

ROOF TERRACE R-55.7

1 paver
2 acrylic roofing
3 4-in tapered foil-faced polyiso
4 3/4-in plywood deck
5 5-in medium-density foam
6 3x10 rafters
7 furring strips
8 GWB

FRONT WALL R-30.4

1 StoTherm Lotusan NExT classic
2 3-in EPS
3 ThoroSeal concrete and masonry sealer
4 12-in existing masonry
5 2-in medium-density foam
6 2 1/2-in medium-density foam between studs
7 GWB

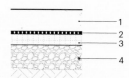

SLAB R-11.2

1 4-in concrete slab
2 15 mm poly air and vapor barrier
3 2-in XPS
4 compacted granular capillary break

174 GRAND

LoadingDock5

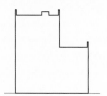

OPPOSITE: Autoclaved aerated concrete units are installed around the parapet to provide a thermal break.

Project location	Brooklyn, NY
Climate zone	mixed humid
Heating degree days	4910°F·days/yr (2728 K·days/yr)
Cooling degree days	1052°F·days/yr (584 K·days/yr)
Treated-floor area	1554 ft² (144 m²)
Airtightness	1.2 ACH at 50 Pa
Number of blower-door tests	2
Primary energy demand	n/a
Wall R-value and U-value	R-33.2, U=0.030 btu/ft²·hr·°F (0.171W/m²·K)
Roof R-value and U-value	R-48.5, U=0.021 btu/ft²·hr·°F (0.117W/m²·K)
Floor R-value and U-value	R-1.8, U=0.565 btu/ft²·hr·°F (3.208W/m²·K)
Window U-value (installed)	0.13 btu/ft²·hr·°F (0.72W/m²·K)
Space-heating demand	4.1 kbtu/ft²·yr (13.0 kWh/m²·yr)
Space-cooling demand	3.2 kbtu/ft²·yr (10.0 kWh/m²·yr)
Heating-equipment type	air-source heat pump
Heating-equipment efficiency	10.0 HSPF; 2.93 COP
Cooling-equipment type	air-source heat pump
Cooling-equipment efficiency	26 HSPF; 7.62 COP
Hot-water-equipment type	heat pump
Hot-water-equipment efficiency	1.58 Energy Factor; 1.58 COP
Ventilation-system type	HRV
Ventilation-system efficiency	84%
Renewable-energy systems	none

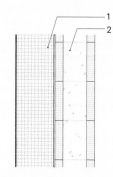

ROOF R-48.5

1 soil
2 moisture barrier
3 10-in polyiso
4 concrete slab on steel pan

WALL R-33.2

1 7-in EPS with acrylic stucco
2 8-in CMU primed and painted

FIRST FLOOR

1 concrete slab on steel pan

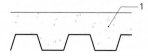

ORIENT STUDIO

Ryall Porter Sheridan Architects

OPPOSITE: Dense-packed cellulose between the wooden framing bays and an intelligent membrane with taped seams in the ceiling thoroughly insulate the building.

Project location	Orient, NY
Climate zone	mixed humid
Heating degree days	5647°F·days/yr (3137 K·days/yr)
Cooling degree days	706°F·days/yr (392 K·days/yr)
Treated-floor area	2405 ft² (223 m²)
Airtightness	0.6 ACH at 50 Pa
Number of blower-door tests	12
Primary energy demand	27.9 kbtu/ft²·yr (88.0 kWh/m²·yr)
Wall R-value and U-value	R-44, U = 0.023 btu/ft²·hr·°F (0.129W/m²·K)
Roof R-value and U-value	R-72, U = 0.014 btu/ft²·hr·°F (0.079W/m²·K)
Floor R-value and U-value	R-57, U = 0.018 btu/ft²·hr·°F (0.100W/m²·K)
Window U-value (installed)	0.15 btu/ft²·hr·°F (0.86W/m²·K)
Space-heating demand	3.8 kbtu/ft²·yr (12.0 kWh/m²·yr)
Space-cooling demand	3.2 kbtu/ft²·yr (10.0 kWh/m²·yr)
Heating-equipment type	air-source heat pump
Heating-equipment efficiency	7.7 HSPF; 2.26 COP
Cooling-equipment type	air-source heat pump
Cooling-equipment efficiency	13 HSPF; 3.81 COP
Hot-water-equipment type	electric tankless
Hot-water-equipment efficiency	0.995 Energy Factor; 0.995 COP
Ventilation-system type	HRV
Ventilation-system efficiency	81%
Renewable-energy systems	4kW PV

ROOF R-72

1 white EPDM roofing membrane
2 6-in site framed mineral wool SIPs
3 18-in TJIs with cellulose
4 5/8-in GWB

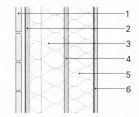

WALL R-44

1 1 1/4-in reclaimed rainscreen
2 black building wrap
3 stud wall with cellulose
4 1/2-in plywood with taped seams
5 2x6 stud wall with cellulose
6 5/8-in GWB

FLOOR R-57

1 Two layers of 3/4-in painted plywood floor
2 18-in TJI floor joists with cellulose
3 3/8-in OSB

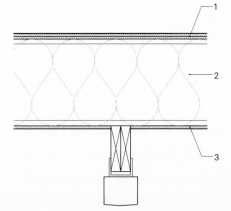

WESTPORT HOUSE

Ken Levenson and Doug Mcdonald

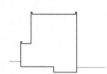

OPPOSITE: Two layers of FOAMGLAS blocks (six and four inches thick) were adhered to the original concrete facade and sealed with bitumen at the joints. The windows were set on a pressure-treated wood ledger within the exterior-insulation layer and sealed with tape for airtightness.

Project location	Westport, CT
Climate zone	cold
Heating degree days	5663°F·days/yr (3146 K·days/yr)
Cooling degree days	825°F·days/yr (458 K·days/yr)
Treated-floor area	3251 ft² (302 m²)
Airtightness	0.91 ACH at 50 Pa
Number of blower-door tests	4
Primary energy demand	27.3 kbtu/ft²·yr (86.0 kWh/m²·yr)
Wall R-value and U-value	R-38, U=0.026 btu/ft²·hr·°F (0.149W/m²·K)
Roof R-value and U-value	R-70, U=0.014 btu/ft²·hr·°F (0.081W/m²·K)
Floor R-value and U-value	R-21, U=0.048 btu/ft²·hr·°F (0.270W/m²·K)
Window U-value (installed)	0.14 btu/ft²·hr·°F (0.77W/m²·K)
Space-heating demand	6.3 kbtu/ft²·yr (20.0 kWh/m²·yr)
Space-cooling demand	1.3 kbtu/ft²·yr (4.0 kWh/m²·yr)
Heating-equipment type	air-source heat pump
Heating-equipment efficiency	10.2 HSPF; 3.0 COP
Cooling-equipment type	air-source heat pump
Cooling-equipment efficiency	13.3 HSPF; 3.9 COP
Hot-water-equipment type	SHW with electric backup
Hot-water-equipment efficiency	0.92 Energy Factor; 0.92 COP
Ventilation-system type	ERV
Ventilation-system efficiency	82%
Renewable-energy systems	solar hot water

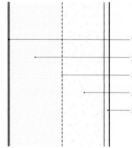

ROOF R-70

1 roofing membrane
2 2-in foam glass
3 air barrier
4 Two layers of 4-in polyiso
5 4-in concrete deck
6 8-in cellulose
7 plaster ceiling

WALL R-38

1 exterior stucco
2 10-in foam glass
3 air barrier
4 8-in concrete wall
5 1-in plaster

SLAB R-21

1 4-in concrete
2 6-in foam glass
3 air barrier

LITTLE COMPTON

ZeroEnergy Design

OPPOSITE:

TOP LEFT: The crew installs wood furring strips for the knotty cedar planks on top of the taped house wrap. All horizontal joints are overlapped by at least six inches.

TOP RIGHT: Wood scissor trusses are visible within the continuous medium-density spray foam.

BOTTOM LEFT: House-wrap returns are visible at the window openings, providing a continuous air seal.

BOTTOM RIGHT: Spray foam is used to seal the gaps around the window frames.

Project location	Little Compton, RI
Climate zone	cold
Heating degree days	5800°F·days/yr (3222 K·days/yr)
Cooling degree days	150°F·days/yr (83 K·days/yr)
Treated-floor area	1209 ft² (112 m²)
Airtightness	0.67 ACH at 50 Pa
Number of blower-door tests	5
Primary energy demand	30.7 kbtu/ft²·yr (96.8 kWh/m²·yr)
Wall R-value and U-value	R-45, U=0.022 btu/ft²·hr·°F (0.126W/m²·K)
Roof R-value and U-value	R-60, U=0.019 btu/ft²·hr·°F (0.095W/m²·K)
Floor R-value and U-value	R-51, U=0.020 btu/ft²·hr·°F (0.111W/m²·K)
Window U-value (installed)	0.16 btu/ft²·hr·°F (0.903W/m²·K)
Space-heating demand	3.81 kbtu/ft²·yr (12.0 kWh/m²·yr)
Space-cooling demand	2.74 kbtu/ft²·yr (8.6 kWh/m²·yr)
Heating-equipment type	air-source heat pump
Heating-equipment efficiency	9.0 HSPF; 2.64 COP
Cooling-equipment type	air-source heat pump
Cooling-equipment efficiency	15 HSPF; 4.4 COP
Hot-water-equipment type	heat pump
Hot-water-equipment efficiency	2.35 Energy Factor; 2.35 COP
Ventilation-system type	HRV
Ventilation-system efficiency	83%
Renewable-energy systems	none

ROOF R-60

1 1x8 knotty cedar planks over aluminum rails
2 asphalt-shingle roofing on waterproofing
3 5/8-in sheathing
4 4-in XPS
5 9-in medium-density foam
6 1/2-in GWB

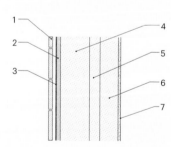

WALL R-45

1 1x6 knotty cedar siding on 1x3 furring strips
2 15/32-in plywood sheathing
3 house-wrap drainage plane
4 2x6 outer stud wall with 7 1/2-in medium density foam
5 2-in cavity filled with medium-density spray foam
6 2x4 nonstructural interior wall with cellulose
7 1/2-in GWB

SLAB R-51

1 4-in concrete slab
2 15 mm poly air barrier
3 10-in XPS
4 grit and crushed stone
5 ground

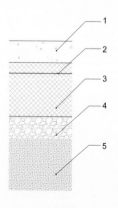

FREEMAN HOUSE

BriggsKnowles A+D

OPPOSITE: The exterior house wrap and insulated interior cavities during TJI framing

Project location	Freeman, ME
Climate zone	cold
Heating degree days	7521˚F·days/yr (4178 K·days/yr)
Cooling degree days	387˚F·days/yr (215 K·days/yr)
Treated-floor area	1244 ft² (116 m²)
Airtightness	0.48 ACH at 50 Pa
Number of blower-door tests	1
Primary energy demand	38.0 kbtu/ft²·yr (119.9 kWh/m²·yr)
Wall R-value and U-value	R-50, U=0.020 btu/ft²·hr·˚F (0.114W/m²·K)
Roof R-value and U-value	R-60, U=0.017 btu/ft²·hr·˚F (0.095W/m²·K)
Floor R-value and U-value	R-70, U=0.014 btu/ ft²·hr·˚F (0.081W/m²·K)
Window U-value (installed)	n/a
Space-heating demand	8.42 kbtu/ft²·yr (26.6 kWh/m²·yr)
Space-cooling demand	0.31 kbtu/ft²·yr (1.0 kWh/m²·yr)
Heating-equipment type	existing
Heating-equipment efficiency	n/a
Cooling-equipment type	n/a
Cooling-equipment efficiency	n/a
Hot-water-equipment type	n/a
Hot-water-equipment efficiency	n/a
Ventilation-system type	ERV
Ventilation-system efficiency	83%
Renewable-energy systems	wind turbine planned

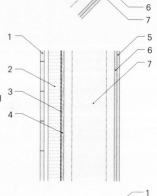

ROOF R-60

1 standing seam metal roof
2 Two layers 1x strapping
3 2 1/2-in EPS board
4 typar building wrap over 3/4-in OSB
5 11 7/8-in TJIs at 24-in open cell with cellulose
6 typar building wrap over 3/4-in OSB
7 1/2-in GWB

WALL R-50

1 T&G red cedar clapboard on vertical furring strips
2 2 1/2-in EPS board
3 vapor barrier
4 1/2-in structural fiber board
5 1/2-in GWB
6 1/2-in OSB
7 9 1/2-in TJIs at 24-in open cell with cellulose

SLAB

1 4-in concrete floor slab
2 6x6–10/10 wwf, center of slab
3 vapor barrier
4 16-in EPS board
5 4-in crushed stone
6 compacted fill continued to footing

VOGEL HOUSE

Diethelm & Spillmann Architekten

OPPOSITE: A concrete block makes up the house's core, with an insulated wooden shell forming the exterior roof, walls, and cantilevered floor.

Project location	Mostelberg, Switzerland
Climate zone	alpine foothills
Heating degree days	7560°F·days/yr (4200 K·days/yr)
Cooling degree days	n/a
Treated-floor area	2131 ft² (198 m²)
Airtightness	0.58 ACH at 50 Pa
Number of blower-door tests	1
Primary energy demand	8.7 kbtu/ft²·yr (27.4 kWh/m²·yr)
Wall R-value and U-value	R-51.6, U = 0.019 btu/ft²·hr·°F (0.110W/m²·K)
Roof R-value and U-value	R-63.1, U = 0.016 btu/ft²·hr·°F (0.090W/m²·K)
Floor R-value and U-value	R-47.3, U = 0.021 btu/ft²·hr·°F (0.120W/m²·K)
Window U-value (installed)	0.14 btu/ft²·hr·°F (0.77W/m²·K)
Space-heating demand	7.23 kbtu/ft²·yr (22.8 kWh/m²·yr)
Space-cooling demand	0.0 kbtu/ft²·yr (0.0 kWh/m²·yr)
Heating-equipment type	solar hot water with wood backup
Heating-equipment efficiency	0.75 HSPF; 0.75 COP
Cooling-equipment type	none
Cooling-equipment efficiency	n/a
Hot-water-equipment type	SHW with electric backup
Hot-water-equipment efficiency	0.9 Energy Factor; 0.9 COP
Ventilation-system type	HRV
Ventilation-system efficiency	73%
Renewable-energy systems	solar hot water; 8kW PV

ROOF R-63.1

1 10 mm double-bitumen sheeting
2 15 mm fireproof board
3 27 mm boarding
4 80 mm battens/air space
5 3 mm waterproofing membrane
6 35 mm block-wood plate
7 420 mm insulation
8 35 mm larch block-wood plate

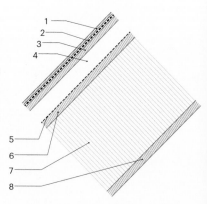

WALL R-51.6

1 19 mm painted spruce cladding
2 30 mm battens/air space
3 16 mm boarding
4 340 mm wood structure and insulation at cavity
5 35 mm larch block-wood plate

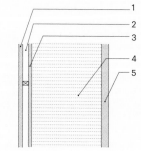

FIRST FLOOR R-47.3

1 250 mm concrete slab
2 280 mm insulation
3 35 mm larch block-wood plate

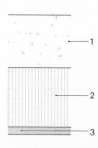

RAINBOW DUPLEX

Marken Projects and Durfeld Constructors

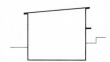

OPPOSITE: A preassembled, two-foot-thick TJI wood-flooring panel with blown cellulose is craned and set in place.

Project location	Whistler, Canada
Climate zone	Canadian Zone B
Heating degree days	6970°F·days/yr (3872 K·days/yr)
Cooling degree days	405°F·days/yr (225 K·days/yr)
Treated-floor area	8444 ft² (784 m²)
Airtightness	0.25 ACH at 50 Pa
Number of blower-door tests	3
Primary energy demand	33.3 kbtu/ft²·yr (105.0 kWh/m²·yr)
Wall R-value and U-value	R-47, U=0.021 btu/ft²·hr·°F (0.121W/m²·K)
Roof R-value and U-value	R-60, U=0.017 btu/ft²·hr·°F (0.095W/m²·K)
Floor R-value and U-value	R-80, U=0.013 btu/ft²·hr·°F (0.071W/m²·K)
Window U-value (installed)	0.14 btu/ft²·hr·°F (0.77W/m²·K)
Space-heating demand	4.6 kbtu/ft²·yr (14.6 kWh/m²·yr)
Space-cooling demand	0.9 kbtu/ft²·yr (2.9 kWh/m²·yr)
Heating-equipment type	air-source heat pump
Heating-equipment efficiency	9.0 HSPF; 2.64 COP
Cooling-equipment type	air-source heat pump
Cooling-equipment efficiency	15.0 HSPF; 4.4 COP
Hot-water-equipment type	solar hot water
Hot-water-equipment efficiency	n/a
Ventilation-system type	HRV
Ventilation-system efficiency	92%
Renewable-energy systems	solar hot water

ROOF R-60

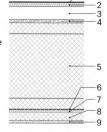

1 waterproofing layer
2 OSB 19 mm Edge Gold
3 ventilated cavity 2x6 framing and waterproof membrane
4 16 mm diffusion board
5 TJIs at 24-in open cell with cellulose
6 polyethylene air-and-vapor barrier
7 15 mm OSB taped airtight
8 service space framing with mineral wool
9 12 mm GWB

WALL R-47

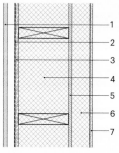

1 19 mm cedar on hardie board
2 building paper
3 16 mm diffusion board
4 235 mm studs at 16-in open cell with cellulose
5 15 mm OSB taped airtight
6 89 mm service space framing with mineral wool
7 12 mm GWB

SLAB R-80

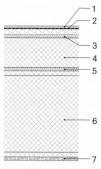

1 10 mm hardwood floor
2 underlayer
3 15 mm OSB
4 140 mm service space framing with mineral wool
5 15 mm OSB taped airtight
6 406 mm TJIs at 24-in open cell with mineral wool
7 16 mm diffusion board

TEXTILE HOUSE

BLAF Architecten

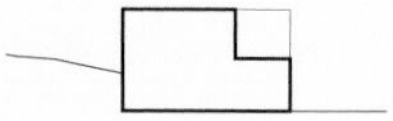

OPPOSITE: Taped window openings within the exterior wooden framing are visible in blue, with the fiber-fabric facade behind.

Project location	Asse, Belgium
Climate zone	temperate maritime climate
Heating degree days	5211°F·days/yr (2895 K·days/yr)
Cooling degree days	140°F·days/yr (78 K·days/yr)
Treated-floor area	1981 ft² (184 m²)
Airtightness	0.3 ACH at 50 Pa
Number of blower-door tests	1
Primary energy demand	n/a
Wall R-value and U-value	R-47.7, U=0.021 btu/ft²·hr·°F (0.119W/m²·K)
Roof R-value and U-value	R-52.6, U=0.019 btu/ft²·hr·°F (0.108W/m²·K)
Floor R-value and U-value	R-49, U=0.020 btu/ft²·hr·°F (0.116W/m²·K)
Window U-value (installed)	0.13 btu/ft²·hr·°F (0.75W/m²·K)
Space-heating demand	4.4 kbtu/ft²·yr (14.0 kWh/m²·yr)
Space-cooling demand	n/a
Heating-equipment type	air-source heat pump
Heating-equipment efficiency	13.5 HSPF; 3.95 COP
Cooling-equipment type	Cooling equipment type: none
Cooling-equipment efficiency	n/a
Hot-water-equipment type	heat pump
Hot-water-equipment efficiency	3.95 Energy Factor; 3.95 COP
Ventilation-system type	HRV
Ventilation-system efficiency	78%
Renewable-energy systems	8.4kW PV

ROOF R-52.6

1 EPDM sealant
2 2x100 mm polyiso
3 insulating mortar
4 200 mm concrete

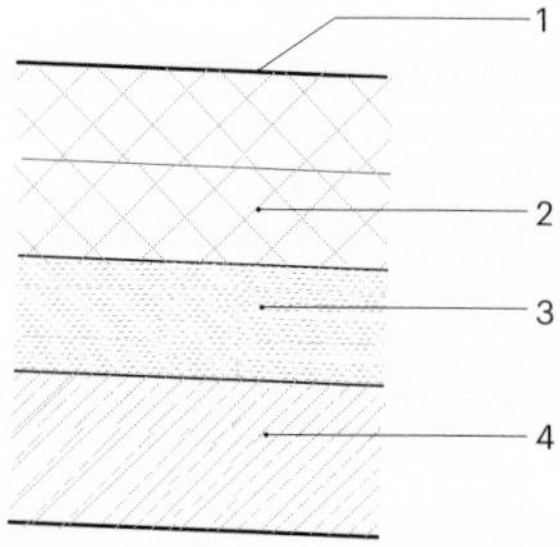

WALL R-47.7

1 masonry units
2 380 mm timber frame with cellulose
3 20 mm wood-fiberboard insulation with air cavity
4 glass-fiber textile

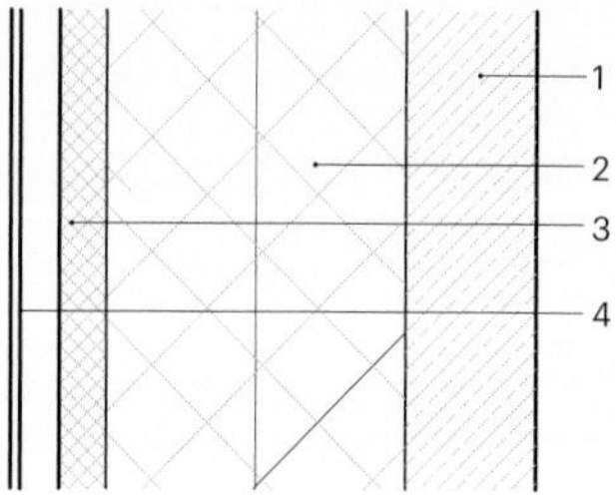

SLAB R-49

1 topping screed
2 insulation
3 200 mm cast concrete
4 Two layers XPS
5 concrete
6 compacted rock fill

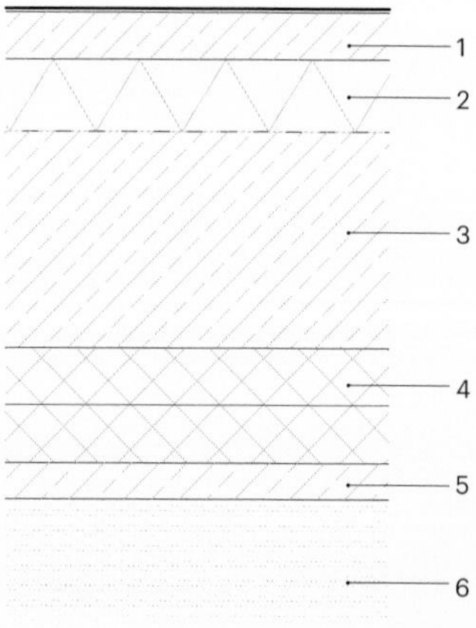

CARRAIG RIDGE PROJECT

Olson Kundig Architects

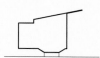

OPPOSITE: It was necessary to balance many criteria to ensure maximum glazing that would also achieve the highest energy performance.

Project location	Ghost Lake, Canada
Climate zone	very cold
Heating degree days	9154°F·days/yr (5086 K·days/yr)
Cooling degree days	67°F·days/yr (37 K·days/yr)
Treated-floor area	1005 ft² (93 m²)
Airtightness	0.6 ACH at 50 Pa (designed)
Number of blower-door tests	n/a
Primary energy demand	28.3 kbtu/ft²·yr (89.3 kWh/m²·yr)
Wall R-value and U-value	R-40, U=0.025 btu/ft²·hr·°F (0.142W/m²·K)
Roof R-value and U-value	R-40, U=0.025 btu/ft²·hr·°F (0.142W/m²·K)
Floor R-value and U-value	R-40, U=0.025 btu/ft²·hr·°F (0.142W/m²·K)
Window U-value (installed)	0.09 btu/ft²·hr·°F (0.50W/m²·K)
Space-heating demand	3.13 kbtu/ft²·yr (9.9 kWh/m²·yr)
Space-cooling demand	4.32 kbtu/ft²·yr (13.6 kWh/m²·yr)
Heating-equipment type	ground-source heat pump
Heating-equipment efficiency	10.2 HSPF; 3.0 COP
Cooling-equipment type	ground-source heat pump
Cooling-equipment efficiency	23.9 HSPF; 7.0 COP
Hot-water-equipment type	ground-source heat pump
Hot-water-equipment efficiency	1.5 Energy Factor; 1.5 COP
Ventilation-system type	ERV
Ventilation-system efficiency	83%
Renewable-energy systems	1.9kW PV

ROOF R-40

1 weathering-steel roof panel
2 fiber-glass framing attachment
3 closed-cell spray foam
4 light gauge metal framing
5 furring
6 1/2-in plywood

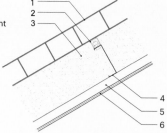

WALL R-40

1 weathering-steel wall panel
2 fiber-glass framing attachment
3 closed-cell spray foam
4 light gauge metal framing
5 furring
6 1/2-in plywood

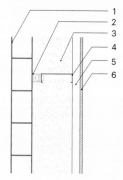

SLAB R-40

1 concrete topping
2 concrete hollow-core plank
3 closed-cell spray foam
4 air space/thermally isolated
  cladding support
5 weathered-steel cladding

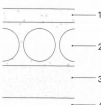

heat loss or gain by using high levels of insulation and airtightness. Superinsulated systems typically include levels of insulation with R-40 to R-60 walls and roofs, insulation continuity, airtight construction, and an HRV system for fresh air supply.

THERM. A two-dimensional heat-transfer modeling program developed by the Lawrence Berkeley National Laboratory to simulate heat flow through an assembly.

zero energy building. Also known as a *zero net energy (ZNE) building*, *nearly zero energy building (NZEB)*, or *net zero building*. Zero energy describes a building with zero net energy consumption and zero carbon emissions annually. Zero energy buildings can be independent from the energy grid. Energy is harvested on-site—usually through-solar and wind-energy-producing technologies—while the energy demand of these buildings is generally reduced through the use of efficient HVAC and lighting systems.

Units

ACH. An abbreviation for *air changes per hour*. A measure of how many times the air within a defined space is replaced per hour.

AFUE. An abbreviation for *annual fuel utilization efficiency*. This is the efficiency measure of natural-gas, propane, and oil-heating appliances. It is a ratio of the delivered heat energy to the energy content of the incoming fuel. An AFUE of 0.95 indicates that 95% of the fuel energy is delivered to the house in the form of heat energy.

BTU. An abbreviation for *British thermal units*. A unit of heat energy defined as the amount of heat required to raise the temperature of one pound of liquid water by one degree Fahrenheit at a constant pressure of one Atmosphere.

coefficient of performance. A measure of the efficiency of heating, cooling, or domestic hot-water equipment. It's a measure of the ratio of heat output (from the equipment) to energy input (to the equipment). Equipment with an efficiency of 100% (typical for electric resistance heating) has a COP of 1. Equipment with an efficiency of 80% (typical of a noncondensing combustion appliance) has a COP of 0.8. Air-source heat pumps have a COP of 2.2 to 3.0, indicating 220–300% efficiency. This seemingly impossible performance is due to the fact that the heat provided by the heat pump is extracted both from outdoor-air thermal energy and from electrical energy (electricity) provided to the unit. Only the electrical energy provided to the unit is factored into the COP formula.

HSPF. An abbreviation for *heating seasonal performance factor*, an efficiency rating for air-source heat pumps. The measurement accounts for varying outdoor conditions and is intended to represent a year-round efficiency since air-source heat-pump efficiencies will change as outdoor air conditions change.

perm value. A unit measuring permeability: the rate of water-vapor transmission given a certain differential in partial pressure on either side of a material or membrane. The US perm value is defined as one grain of water vapor per house, per square foot, per inch of mercury.

R-value (hr·ft^2·°F/BTU). The thermal resistance of a building envelope: the amount of energy transfer (BTU/hr) resisted by one square foot (ft^2) of the envelope, for every one degree Fahrenheit (°F) difference between the inside and outside temperature, per hour.

SEER. An abbreviation for *seasonal energy efficiency rating*, an efficiency rating for air-conditioning equipment. The measurement accounts for varying outdoor conditions and is intended to represent a year-round efficiency since air-conditioner efficiencies will change as outdoor-air conditions change.

SHGC. An abbreviation for *solar heat gain coefficient*. The fraction of incident solar radiation admitted through a window and subsequently released inward. SHGC is expressed as a number between 0 and 1. The lower a window's SHGC, the less solar heat it transmits to the interior of a building.

U-value (W/m^2·K). Also known as *U-factor*. Describes the thermal transmittance of a building envelope or the heat loss of a window assembly. The amount of energy lost in watts (W) through one square meter (m^2) of the envelope, for every one degree Kelvin (K) difference between the inside and outside temperature, per hour.

PROJECT CREDITS

KAMAKURA
Key Architects

Key Architects:
Miwa Mori, partner
Joerg Heil, partner

General contractor: Kenchikusya Co, Ltd.
Solar installer: Ecomo Ltd.

PRESCOTT HOUSE
Studio 804

Studio 804:
Executive director: Dan Rockhill
Student participants: C.J. Armstrong, Elizabeth
    Beckerle, Joshua Brown, William Doran, Colleen
    Driver, Laura Foster, Joel Garcia, Tyler Harrelson,
    Lauren Hickman, Aaron Jensen, Matthew
    Johnson, Daniel Lipscomb, Daniel Matchett,
    Jennifer Mayfield, Katherine Morell, Tye Zehner

General contractor: Studio 804
Engineer: Norton & Schmidt
Passive House consultant: Ryan Abendroth, Passive
    Energy Designs

TWO POINT FIVE
ISA and Postgreen

100K House
Interface Studio Architects:
Brian Phillips, principal
Daryn Edwards, principal
May Narisaranukul, project manager
Morgan Ellig, designer
Justin Diles, designer

Developer: Postgreen Homes
General contractor: Manor Hill Construction
Structural engineer: Larsen and Landis
LEED/Energy Star consultant: MaGrann Associates

Passive House
Interface Studio Architects:
Brian Phillips, principal
Daryn Edwards, principal

Kara Medow, project manager
Morgan Ellig, designer

Developer: Postgreen Homes
General contractor: Postgreen Homes
Structural engineer: Larsen and Landis
Passive House consultant: E-co Lab

Skinny House
Interface Studio Architects:
Brian Phillips, principal
Daryn Edwards, principal
Kara Medow, project manager

Developer: Postgreen Homes
General contractor: Hybrid Construction
Structural engineer: Larsen and Landis

Two Point Five
Interface Studio Architects:
Brian Phillips, principal
Daryn Edwards, principal
Kara Medow, project manager

Developer: Postgreen Homes
General contractor: Hybrid Construction
Structural engineer: Larsen and Landis
LEED/Energy Star consultant: MaGrann Associates

BELFIELD
Onion Flats

Developer: Belfield Avenue Townhouse Development
    and Onion Flats
Architect: Onion Flats as Plumbob
General contractor: Onion Flats as Jig
Modular builder: Onion Flats as BLOX Sustainable
    Building Systems
Mechanical engineer: DCM Architecture &
    Engineering

TIGHTHOUSE
Fabrica718

Fabrica718:
Julie Torres Moskovitz, founder
Project team: Minyoung Song, Kim Letven, Natalya
    Egon, Corey Yurkovich, Michael Vanreusel, Jade Yang

Architect of record: Melissa Cicetti, studio Cicetti
General contractor: WM Dorvillier & Comp
Structural engineer: Chris Anastos, Anastos
    Engineering
Mechanical engineer: Nino D'Antonio, D'Antonio
    Consulting Engineers
Passive House consultant: Jordan Goldman,
    ZeroEnergy Design
Furniture: Vitra, Knoll Studio, Nanimarquina, and Kea
    Carpets

174 GRAND
LoadingDock5

LoadingDock5:
Sam Bargetz, Werner Morath, partners

General contractor: LoadingDock5
Structural engineer: Murray Engineering
Passive House consultant: David White, Right
    Environments

ORIENT STUDIO
Ryall Porter Sheridan Architects

Ryall Porter Sheridan Architects:
William Ryall, principal
John Buckley, project designer

General contractor: Phil Manuele
Structural engineer: Dewhurst Macfarlane and
    Partners
Solar PV installer: Sunstream USA
Passive House consultant: David White, Right
    Environments

WESTPORT HOUSE
Ken Levenson and Doug Mcdonald

Ken Levenson Architect:
Ken Levenson, principal
Tina Diep, project architect

Designer and general contractor: Doug Mcdonald
Passive House consultant: Greg Duncan

LITTLE COMPTON
ZeroEnergy Design

ZeroEnergy Design:
Jordan Goldman, HVAC design and Passive House
    consulting
Stephanie Horowitz, design and Passive House
    consulting
Adam Prince, LEED-H Green Rater

General contractor: Aedi Construction

HUDSON PASSIVE PROJECT
Dennis Wedlick Architect

Dennis Wedlick Architect:
Dennis Wedlick, principal
Alan Barlis, principal
Brian Marsh, associate
Anna Klein, staff architect
Adriana Gerbig, interior designer
Nicole Bacani, marketing

General contractor: Bill Stratton Building
Mechanical engineer: CDH Energy
Structural engineer: John Treybal, VTF Engineering
    Ventures
Passive House consultant/building science team:
    The Levy Partnership

R-HOUSE
Architecture Research Office and Della Valle
    Bernheimer

Stephen Cassell and Adam Yarinsky, principals
Megumi Tamanaha, associate
Design team: Melissa Eckerman, Jane Lea, Neil Patel,
    Anne-Marie Singer

Della Valle Bernheimer:
Andrew Bernheimer and Jared Della Valle, partners
Garrick Jones, associate
Design team: Lara Shihab Eldin, Janine Soper

Senior engineer and project manager: David White
Structural engineer: Guy Nordenson and Associates
    Structural Engineers
Passive House consultant: Transsolar Climate
    Engineering

FREEMAN HOUSE
BriggsKnowles A+D

BriggsKnowles A+D:
Laura Briggs, principal
Jonathan Knowles, principal
Obinna Elechi, representation
Ann-Marie Fallon, energy analysis
Jason Lim, designer

General contractor: Sebastian and Hezekiah Tooker,
    Sebastian Tooker Construction
Mechanical engineer: Buddy Kempton, Mountain
    Mechanical
Lighting and fixture design: Derek Porter, Derek
    Porter Studio
Passive House consultant: Katrin Klingenberg, PHIUS

VOGEL HOUSE
Diethelm & Spillmann Architekten

Diethelm & Spillmann Architekten:
Daniel Spillmann, partner

General contractor: Schnuriger Bau
Structural engineer: Pius Schuler AG
Technical building systems: Hassig-sustech
Building physicist: Raumanzug
Electrical engineer: Elprom AG

BAMBOO HOUSE
Karawitz Architecture

Karawitz Architecture:
Milena Karanesheva, principal
Mischa Witzmann, principal
Solares Bauen, thermal engineer

Civil engineer consultant for wooden structure:
    DI Eisenhauer
Civil engineer consultant for concrete structure:
    Philippe Buchet
Airtightness consultant: Manexi

AUSTRIA HOUSE
Treberspurg & Partner Architekten

Treberspurg & Partner Architekten:
Martin Treberspurg, Christoph Treberspurg, Johana
    Treberspurg, Wolfgang Csenar, partners

General contractor, Austria: Sohm Holzbautechnik
General contractor, Canada: Durfeld Constructors
Project coordination, Austria: Erich Reiner
Project coordination and marketing, Canada:
    sea to sky consulting

RAINBOW DUPLEX
Marken Projects and Durfeld Constructors

Architect: Marken Projects
General contractor/Developer: Durfeld Constructors
Engineer: Equilibrium Consulting
Prefabricated envelope: BC Passive House
PPHPP analysis: Natalie Leonard

TEXTILE HOUSE
BLAF Architecten

BLAF Architecten:
Lieven Nijs, Barbara Oelbrandt, Bart Vanden
    Driessche

General contractor: Frank Haentjens, CDS; Philippe
    Bontinck, bvba; Luc Martens
Technical contractors: Flidais (HVAC), Vamitech
    (Electrician)

CARRAIG RIDGE PROJECT
Olson Kundig Architects

Olson Kundig Architects:
Design principals: Les Eerkes, Steven Rainville
Staff: Angus McGregor, Derek Santo
Research: Wei Yan
Design mentor: Tom Kundig

Mechanical engineer/Passive House consultant:
    ReNü Building Science Inc.
Structural engineer: Magnusson Klemencic
    Associates
Glass consultant: Front

ILLUSTRATION CREDITS